Unity in Shakespearian

Tragedy

Unity in Shakespearian Tragedy

Tragedy

The Interplay of Theme and Character

By Brents Stirling

Columbia University Press
New York, 1956

To My Mother and Father

Acknowledgments

WHATEVER originality it
may have, a study of Shakespeare is at once a recognition
and a modification of previous studies. I wish to acknowledge especially the work of E. E. Stoll, Lily B. Campbell,
E. M. W. Tillyard, O. J. Campbell, G. R. Elliott, G. Wilson Knight, Willard Farnham, Moody Prior, Robert Heilman, and Francis Fergusson. They and others equally di-
verse have provided information, interpretation, and controversy upon which I have drawn. The Shakespearian
world is a large one which contains every point of view
save the orthodox, and it is notable that few in that world
would want to change it. I am also happy to remember the
valuable help of my students and colleagues at the University of Washington. And to Alice Stirling who typed
and read the manuscript not once but several times I am
more indebted than she knows.

Anyone who attempts a close study of the Shakespearian
text will sometimes duplicate independently the observations of other writers. I have tried to acknowledge all such
material which is not yet part of the public domain, but I
may have missed some of it. Perhaps someday there will
be an effective indexing of the great mass of Shakespeare
studies by subject as well as by title.

I wish to note that some of my essays, now extensively revised, appeared originally in the *Shakespeare Quarterly*, the *Modern Language Quarterly*, and *PMLA*.

The Shakespearian text used here is from the edition of W. A. Neilson and C. J. Hill, *The Complete Plays and Poems of William Shakespeare* (Boston: Houghton Mifflin Co., 1942).

A final acknowledgment is due the Agnes H. Anderson Research Fund of the University of Washington. From this source has come a generous grant in aid of publication, for which I am most grateful.

BRENTS STIRLING

Seattle, Washington
November 16, 1955

Contents

Unity in Shakespearian

Tragedy

i. Introduction

ALTHOUGH the chapters of this book deal with different plays and their special problems, they have a subject in common. Whatever the treatment of a play, the question will be one of theme and its relation to structure and motivation. Structure will simply mean interconnection between elements or qualities. Motivation will mean the creation of a state of mind which governs not only a character but the play of which he is a part. A typical theme which will be considered is drawn from the "recorder" passage which expresses Hamlet's resentment at being played like a simple pipe. With attention to structure, this idea is followed through serious and comic variations from its introduction to its final statement. With reference to motivation, it is considered both as a means of revealing Hamlet's character and as a psychological principle reflected throughout the play. The treatment of thematic elements in other plays will be similar.

The word "theme" will have meanings which occasionally differ, and in the chapter on *Macbeth* it will be used in a way which probably departs from standard practice. I dislike such terms as "motif," "thread," or "strand," and I do not believe there is anything confusing about using a single term to describe things which differ only in nonessentials. The elements in *Macbeth* which are called themes are not exactly like the elements of *Othello* which are given the same name, but their significance is the same in our problem. In any event, "theme" will never mean *the* theme; I have no wish to rule out alternative interpretation or to imply that Shakespeare obtained unity by narrowing his range.

In the essays which follow I have never consciously overlooked Elizabethan points of view. Some themes I describe, such as the one expressed by the "passion's slave" lines in *Hamlet*, will be understood as common to Shakespeare's time. Certain others are not so clearly historical, but when I have found these in the plays I have tried to show that they are supported by Shakespeare's plain and repeated emphasis. Among such themes are reputation in *Othello*, ritual dedication in *Julius Caesar*, and "raptness" in *Macbeth*.

In other words, I have tried to avoid being antihistorical, but on occasion I have probably been nonhistorical, which may be a lesser offense. If we assume some complexity in Shakespeare's art and set out to describe it, we are bound to risk anachronism in our effort to enlarge history. To evade the risk by falling back upon Elizabethan convention is simply to take chances of another kind, for norms of performance obscure the past as effectively as they illuminate it. And in applying such norms to Shakespeare there are more than ordinary chances of missing Elizabethan individuality—a platitude, surely, but perhaps a serviceable one.

If we attempt to discover a playwright more historical than the Shakespeare of sixteenth-century convention, internal evidence from the plays themselves must provide our information, and it will be found least subjective when based upon the various forms of dramatic emphasis.[1] Such evidence, of course, has its own possibilities of misuse. For example, any play will show design or structure, and if the problem is one of theme nothing is more tempting than to fit theme to structure and then find it emphasized because it follows a pattern. Whether or not a good method is thus misapplied will sometimes be the question, so that the final test may have to be the difficult one of discrimination. But this is hardly surprising; in problems either of art or history the test of good judgment has always been good judgment. One can only do his best and invite the help of others.

The internal emphasis of a play is perhaps the best evidence pointing to the nature of a dramatist's work. The problem raised by a part of Cleanth Brooks's essay on *Macbeth* [2] may illustrate this. Without prejudice to his main argument we may consider Mr. Brooks's interpretation of a well-known passage:

> Here lay Duncan,
> His silver skin lac'd with his golden blood;
> And his gash'd stabs look'd like a breach in nature
> For ruin's wasteful entrance; there the murderers
> Steep'd in the colours of their trade, their daggers
> Unmannerly breech'd with gore.

Mr. Brooks relates "breech'd" to a design of clothing imagery which in its larger dimensions is hard to ignore. How shall we judge this part of his interpretation? Some literary

---

[1] A reliance upon emphasis is a reliance upon matters which a perceptive spectator or reader can feel are "carried" or consistently borne out by the play. For reasons apparent to anyone who has faced the problem, such a criterion does not establish "objectivity," an unattainable goal in value judgments. But it discourages egocentric judgment which exploits a critic's sensibilities at the expense of the object before him.

[2] "The Naked Babe and the Cloak of Manliness," in *The Well Wrought Urn* (New York, 1947), pp. 21–46.

historians may object to it by saying that Shakespeare as a dramatist of his age was not concerned with "image patterns" extending throughout a play, and that once we forget this *Macbeth* becomes anything the critic wants to make of it. Neither part of the objection is justified, for to appraise Shakespeare by Elizabethan convention begs the question and to say that Mr. Brooks invites relativity probably ignores it. But what happens if we appeal to contextual emphasis? Assuming that Macbeth's reference to daggers "unmannerly breech'd with gore" does involve breeches, the passage is difficult to connect with a scheme of clothes imagery because it comes in a context so immediate and so strong that the suggestion of clothes is displaced, if not overwhelmed. Despite an additional clothing image in the quoted lines (Duncan's skin is "lac'd" with blood), imagery of a competing sort in the surrounding passages absorbs both this and the "breech'd with gore" figure into quite another scheme, the familiar one of bloody daggers in bloody hands [3] which, in turn, is part of the hand-washing design. By any standard of emphasis within the play itself the hand-washing pattern would have to be admitted both as historical and artistic fact. In preferring this interpretation to Mr. Brooks's I do not suggest that a major current of imagery eliminates strong but minor currents; the bloody hands theme can coexist, I believe, with steadily asserted ones such as sleep and darkness which appear with it, but it should overshadow any isolated metaphor, whether or not the latter is "related" to a plan in some other part of the play.

It may be helpful to describe a few of the standards I

[3] This would support Nares's suggestion that "breech" actually means not the scabbard of a dagger but the hilt. See the *Variorum.*

have used in trying to verify a theme or idea and the art which represents it. There is of course the negative one just mentioned in the reference to Mr. Brooks. A common affirmative test is to look for repetition of a subject in parallel form. My interpretations of Henry Bolingbroke and Iago call upon psychological notions of contradiction which may appear modern rather than Elizabethan, so it is reassuring to find in *Richard II* three parallel episodes which present Bolingbroke's contradiction, and in *Othello* two which disclose Iago's. It is also encouraging to discover in *Macbeth* that the thematic pattern surrounding Duncan's death is repeated at the killing of Banquo. Whether in these examples something has been found repeated because its original appearance was assumed, I must leave to the reader.

Because first impressions are likely to be controlling, another familiar sign of emphasis will be the presence of key material in exposition. In *Antony and Cleopatra*, for example, the opening scenes immediately question Antony's claim to tragic stature, and thus they begin the "nobleness of life" as an ironical theme. Similarly, the privacy or "recorder" note in *Hamlet* is suggested at length in the first scene with a ghost impressively "offended" by the watchers who demand its secret. Exposition by itself, however, rarely establishes a theme, and in this respect it is like any other single aspect of a play. The most it can usually offer is a strong beginning.

An additional indication of emphasis is the dramatist's choice of subject for dialogue or situation. In Act I, scene i of *Julius Caesar*, Shakespeare could have had his tribunes rebuke their inferiors in quite general terms, but instead they send the plebs to ceremonies of atonement for their impiety. In scene ii he could have used any of a dozen situations from Plutarch to introduce Caesar and his retinue; yet he chooses the Lupercalian rites. Selection of these possibilities from the many at hand points to a concern for materials that "fit" the ritual killing of Caesar and the ceremonial theme of the tragedy. The example just given actually includes three types of emphasis: selective use of materials, exposition, and cumulative repetition.

Other kinds of dramatic stress are available as evidence, but they need not be described. Choric discourse upon a theme is one of these and the use of thematic material at climactic points is another. The principles of internal evidence in dramatic art are many and various. I wish to make the point, however, that they are not just tools of the historian who wishes to verify ideas and techniques in drama of the past. They are also important to the critic. If we can determine a Shakespearian theme by introductory, selective, climactic, or choric emphasis we are not only able to call it historical; we can begin to see the part it plays in a work of art which, in the worn but honest formula, contains its own emphasis and its own meaning. On this plane the historian and the critic can work to mutual advantage.

If I may be allowed a single plea for "understanding," I should like to advance an old but neglected principle: no interpretation of Shakespeare should be considered as an attempt at completeness, nor should any interpretation be read as denying another with which it is not actually in conflict. If an essay on *Hamlet* seems in its stressing of a part of the play to obscure the whole, the obscuring is often not a fault of the critic but of his readers, who interpret his necessary emphasis as an exclusion of collateral and often very important matters. This is the wrong way to read most criticism, and I hope that no one will find, for example, that my notion of Hamlet's concern for privacy as a motive for his antic disposition is incompatible with Mr. Alexander's excellent idea [4] that Hamlet feigns madness as a medium of honorable disclosure to Claudius that he is the king's adversary. Plural motives do exist, and they can be managed by good dramatists.

Introductions may be either suggestive or discursive, but they should in any event be brief. I should like to add merely that I do not pretend to have discovered such elements in Shakespeare as the ambiguity of Hamlet's antic disposition, the taciturnity of Bolingbroke, or the satirical strain in *Antony and Cleopatra*. My attempted contribution is not so much concerned with Shakespeare's subject matter as with his rendition of it. Some of the themes discussed here are old ones and some are designated for the first time, but whether old or new they are treated as a part of poetic drama.

[4] Peter Alexander, *Hamlet, Father and Son* (Oxford, 1955), pp. 177–82.

ii. *"They stumble that run fast"*

THE unguarded haste of youth as a tragic motive of both Romeo and Juliet appears repeatedly in their lines and in those of characters who describe them. Our common understanding of this [1] needs to be accompanied, however, by an understanding of the haste theme as it marks all aspects of the tragedy. *Romeo and Juliet* is perhaps unique in its clear-cut and consistent expression of theme through character, choric commentary, and action.

The opening scene of the play establishes the pace at which tragic fate will unfold. In little more than a hundred lines the Capulet-Montague feud is introduced with the thumb-biting scene, is extended by infiltration of the gentry, and is dramatically stayed with choric judgment by the Prince of Verona. This quality of events hurrying to a decision is expressed, moreover, by incidental dialogue: in the beginning, Sampson's line, "I strike quickly, being mov'd," and Gregory's response, "But thou art not quickly mov'd to strike," comically introduce the theme of impetuous speed,

[1] For an early recognition of the phenomenon see W. W. Lloyd, *Critical Essays on the Plays of Shakespeare* (London, 1875), pp. 365–67. It is also commonly understood, and accepted here, that "suggestions of a more prolonged action modify the breathless pace of events." See, for example, Raymond Chapman in *Modern Language Review*, XLIV (1949), 372–74.

and at the conclusion of the brawl even the interviews decreed by Escalus appear in terms of dispatch: "You, Capulet, shall go along with me;/ And, Montague, come you this afternoon."

Scene ii now presents haste as a theme governing the betrothal: Capulet declares that Juliet "hath not seen the change of fourteen years" and urges Paris to "let two more summers wither in their pride,/ Ere we may think her ripe to be a bride." From this is derived the well-worn exposition device of tragic irony which points significantly at a misfortune which will come "too soon."

> *Paris.* Younger than she are happy mothers made.
> *Capulet.* And too soon marr'd are those so early made.

In scene iii the headlong quality continues both in plot movement and thematic dialogue. The question is put to Juliet: "Thus then in brief:/ The valiant Paris seeks you for his love./ . . . What say you? Can you love the gentleman?/ This night you shall behold him at our feast." Twenty lines later, the feast is not only shown as imminent but as characterized by the haste and confusion through which comic characters will express the theme. A servant enters:

> Madam, the guests are come, supper serv'd up, you call'd, my young lady ask'd for, the nurse curs'd in the pantry, and everything in extremity. I must hence to wait; I beseech you, follow straight.

Scene iv opens with lines which continue the theme ingeniously in terms of a masking. The maskers reject slow and measured "prologue" entries as "prolixity," and propose to give their performance "and be gone":

Enter ROMEO, MERCUTIO, BENVOLIO, *with five*
or six other MASKERS, TORCH-BEARERS.
Romeo. What, shall this speech be spoke for our excuse?
Or shall we on without apology?
Benvolio. The date is out of such prolixity.
We'll have no Cupid hoodwink'd with a scarf,
Bearing a Tartar's painted bow of lath,
Scaring the ladies like a crow-keeper;
Nor no without-book prologue, faintly spoke
After the prompter, for our entrance;
But let them measure us by what they will,
We'll measure them a measure and be gone.

Here also is the first entry of Mercutio who both as a
character and as a name will point up the quick, the mer-
curial, mood of the play. And now a scene which began
with the maskers as symbols of dispatch ends with a further
thematic turn; a feared lateness of arrival at the feast is first
made suggestive and then direct in disclosing untimeliness
as a tragic theme:

Benvolio. This wind you talk of blows us from ourselves.
Supper is done, and we shall come too late.
Romeo. I fear, too early; for my mind misgives
Some consequence, yet hanging in the stars,
Shall bitterly begin his fearful date
With this night's revels, and expire the term
Of a despised life clos'd in my breast,
By some vile forfeit of untimely death.
But He that hath the steerage of my course
Direct my sail! On, lusty gentlemen!
Benvolio. Strike, drum.   *They march about the stage.*

The theme appears clearly here in exposition which goes
beyond dramatic irony into conscious prophecy, and becomes a formulation of the tragedy itself: in the "con-

sequence yet hanging in the stars" the passage echoes the "star-cross'd lovers" line of the Prologue, and it expresses Christian elements of tragedy through Romeo's reference to his "despised life" and his ascription of "steerage" to God's will. Romeo's lines are thus plainly designed for choric purposes, and any thematic material in them may be taken seriously. So it is notable that the passage arises from a quip implying haste (Benvolio's line) and adds earliness, untimeliness, to the conventional tragic themes of fate, *contemptus mundi,* and divine providence. A concern over exposition as a "validating" factor should not, however, obscure the art by which Shakespeare supports his prophetic lines with dramatic action: as Romeo, sensing untimely death, consigns the steerage of his course to God, his sudden final words, "On, lusty gentlemen!" evoke Benvolio's command, "Strike, drum," and the march about the stage. Choric comment upon speeding fate is thus succeeded instantly by the peremptory drum and a quick-time march of maskers which present the theme in sound and movement.

As scene iv closes with this expression of the haste theme, the next scene continues it with a comic device already noted in scene iii—servants hastily preparing for the feast:

> *First Servant.* Where's Potpan, that he helps not to take away? He shift a trencher! He scrape a trencher!
> *Second Servant.* When good manners shall lie all in one or two men's hands, and they unwash'd too, 'tis a foul thing.
> *First Servant.* Away with the joint-stools, remove the court-cupboard, look to the plate. Good thou, save me a piece of marchpane; and, as thou loves me, let the porter let in Susan Grindstone and Nell. Antony and Potpan!
> *Second Servant.* Ay, boy, ready.

> *First Servant.* You are look'd for and call'd for, ask'd for
> and sought for, in the great chamber.
> *Third Servant.* We cannot be here and there too. Cheerly,
> boys; be brisk a while, and the longer liver take all.

In Elizabethan staging this passage would come immediately
after the close of scene iv and hence would follow Romeo's
speech and the lively exit march begun with Benvolio's
"Strike, drum." Thus, in the sequence, I.iv.104 ff. through
I.v.1–17, actual, physical pace issues from Romeo's lines on
tragic pace, and this in turn is expanded into lines and
action presenting haste on the comic plane. It is also interesting, whether Shakespeare "meant it" or not, that the
servant who ends the passage just quoted comically modifies
Romeo's speech on swift, untimely tragedy: "be brisk a
while, and the longer liver take all."

In the next portion of scene v old Capulet and his kinsman who are met for the feast immediately supplement
the theme with dialogue on the rush of time since their last
masking; over thirty years it has been since the nuptial of
Lucentio whose son's age thus points to the unbelievable
passage of a generation. Plot movement then extends this
statement of theme with a quick sequence composed of
Romeo's first glimpse of Juliet, Tybalt's threat of violence
which is restrained by his uncle, and the meeting of the
lovers which brings discovery that one is a Montague, the
other a Capulet. In attending to verbal expressions of theme
it is easy to forget that plot structure can thus silently do
its work. In *Macbeth*, for example, the compressed action
leading to Duncan's murder parallels the quality of rash
obsession which is so dominant in the lines. The structure of
Romeo and Juliet is similar; from Act I, scene ii onward,

audience attention is centered upon a progressively imminent event, the Capulet feast, which in scene v is suddenly
presented for a casting of the tragic die. Here Romeo and
Juliet meet, their fate becomes implicit in the discovery of
their lineage, and prophetic Death in the person of Tybalt
is barely restrained from a harvest before the seed is planted.
The action itself embodies Romeo's choric lines on fated,
fatal dispatch.

The Prologue of Act II continues the theme in its opening passage,

> Now old Desire doth in his death-bed lie,
> And young Affection gapes to be his heir,

suggestive lines which are translated into action by the
pursuing of Romeo, who "ran this way, and leap'd this
orchard wall." The balcony scene now brings a necessary
lull or resting point in the fast pace, but the famous exchange
between the lovers continues the theme of haste. In II.ii
Juliet implies it:

> My ears have yet not drunk a hundred words
> Of thy tongue's uttering, yet I know the sound.

And her lines presently become explicit:

> Although I joy in thee,
> I have no joy of this contract tonight;
> It is too rash, too unadvis'd, too sudden,
> Too like the lightning, which doth cease to be
> Ere one can say it lightens.

As before, plot supplements thematic statement; events become imminent as calls by the Nurse end the tryst and
induce dialogue which expresses haste compounded with a
desire to linger:

Juliet.   What o'clock to-morrow
   Shall I send to thee?
Romeo.   By the hour of nine.
Juliet. I will not fail; 'tis twenty year till then.
   I have forgot why I did call thee back.
Romeo. Let me stand here till thou remember it.
Juliet. I shall forget, to have thee still stand there,
   Rememb'ring how I love thy company.
Romeo. And I'll still stay, to have thee still forget,
   Forgetting any other home but this.
Juliet. 'Tis almost morning, I would have thee gone;—
   And yet no farther than a wanton's bird. . . .

If it is to give the illusion of pace, episodic action must
have fluidity, a quality Shakespeare maintains here by beginning II.iii on a note carried over from II.ii. Romeo and
Juliet have closed the latter scene with lines on morning and
the haste it brings. Then, as the next one commences, we
hear Friar Laurence:

   The grey-ey'd morn smiles on the frowning night,
   Chequ'ring the eastern clouds with streaks of light,
   And flecked darkness like a drunkard reels
   From forth day's path and Titan's fiery wheels.
   Now, ere the sun advance his burning eye,
   The day to cheer and night's dank dew to dry. . . .

It is important to note that this is the first appearance of
the Friar and that his role is a distinctly prophetic one. After
the lines just quoted he moralizes aptly on tragic symbolism
in the herb which "strain'd from that fair use,/ Revolts from
true birth, stumbling on abuse":

   Virtue itself turns vice, being misapplied;
   And vice sometime's by action dignified.

Then as Romeo silently enters, Friar Laurence produces
the plant which delights when smelled but kills when tasted.

After thus establishing the Friar's role as chorus for the tragedy, Shakespeare then makes him spokesman of the haste theme: his greeting dwells solely upon Romeo's "earliness" and the "distemp'rature" from which it arises:

> *Benedicite!*
> What early tongue so sweet saluteth me?
> Young son, it argues a distempered head
> So soon to bid good morrow to thy bed.
> Care keeps his watch in every old man's eye,
> And where care lodges, sleep will never lie;
> But where unbruised youth with unstuff'd brain
> Doth couch his limbs, there golden sleep doth reign;
> Therefore thy earliness doth me assure
> Thou art up-rous'd with some distemp'rature.

Friar Laurence's thematic moralizing now extends to Rosaline, "so soon forsaken":

> Lo, here upon thy cheek the stain doth sit
> Of an old tear that is not wash'd off yet.

And as scene iii closes, the Friar's admonition by indirection changes to an outright statement of the haste theme:

> *Romeo.* O, let us hence; I stand on sudden haste.
> *Friar.* Wisely and slow; they stumble that run fast.

The next scene presents dialogue between Romeo, Benvolio, and Mercutio, in which an accelerated badinage continues the theme of oppressive haste: at the end of the exchange, as Mercutio complains that his "wits faint" from the quick give-and-take, we hear Romeo exclaiming, "Switch and spurs, switch and spurs, or I'll cry a match," and Mercutio observing, "Nay, if our wits run the wild goose chase, I am done. . . ." Then, as the scene ends with Romeo's urging of speed in arranging the lovers' meeting, we hear the Nurse commanding Peter, "Before and apace."

Again, as Juliet introduces II.v by reference to the over-
due Nurse, there is a lively "run-on" from the exit lines of
one scene to the entry lines of another. Juliet's soliloquy
and the Nurse's appearance then combine to assert the haste
theme fully and impressively:

> The clock struck nine when I did send the nurse;
> In half an hour she promis'd to return.
> Perchance she cannot meet him; that's not so.
> O, she is lame! Love's heralds should be thoughts,
> Which ten times faster glide than the sun's beams
> Driving back shadows over louring hills;
> Therefore do nimble-pinion'd doves draw Love,
> And therefore hath the wind-swift Cupid wings.
> Now is the sun upon the highmost hill
> Of this day's journey, and from nine till twelve
> Is three long hours, yet she is not come.
> Had she affections and warm youthful blood,
> She would be as swift in motion as a ball;
> My words would bandy her to my sweet love,
> And his to me;
> But old folks, marry, feign as they were dead,
> Unwieldy, slow, heavy and pale as lead.

The Nurse enters here with comically labored breathing
(a device also of scene iii) which accompanies her exclama-
tion of "Jesu, what haste!" and the scene shifts back to the
cell of Friar Laurence who plays a "slowing" role opposite
Romeo analogous to the Nurse's role with Juliet. But the
lovers meet in the cell and their marriage is arranged with the
dispatch which is now coloring all aspects of the play; Friar
Laurence speaks:

> Come, come with me, and we will make short work;
> For, by your leaves, you shall not stay alone
> Till Holy Church incorporate two in one.

Act III, scene i now brings the street fight in which
Mercutio is killed, and speed in the action is again accompanied by lines which express the haste theme. Mercutio's
challenge comes in such terms: "Will you pluck your sword
out of his pilcher by the ears? Make haste, lest mine be
about your ears ere it be out." And at Mercutio's death
the lament of Romeo points to the rush of events within a
single hour:

> This gentleman, the Prince's near ally,
> My very friend, hath got this mortal hurt
> In my behalf; my reputation stain'd
> With Tybalt's slander,—Tybalt, that an hour
> Hath been my cousin!

Even the notion of death appears in a metaphor of souls
ascending in quick succession:

> Now, Tybalt, take the "villain" back again
> That late thou gav'st me; for Mercutio's soul
> Is but a little way above our heads,
> Staying for thine. . . .

At this point citizens enter in pursuit which results in an
episode similar to I.i as the Prince, with full retinue, quiets
the disorder and pronounces judgment on it. One might
expect here a speech which would slow the movement, but
at this stage of the play all characters, even those rendering
judicial decrees, are given lines which carry the theme of
immediacy and hurry. Escalus closes the scene:

> And for that offence
> Immediately we do exile him hence.
>
> .   .   .   .
>
> Let Romeo hence in haste,
> Else, when he's found, that hour is his last.

Bear hence this body and attend our will.
Mercy but murders, pardoning those that kill.

Once more, as a scene is closed with the haste theme, the next one is begun on the same note. The transition, moreover, contains irony which has the sudden quality expressed by the action and the imagery. In III.ii Juliet's opening lines succeed the Prince's decree which ends III.i. He has banished Romeo "hence in haste" and Juliet, unaware of this, calls for Romeo's return with all speed and urgency:

Gallop apace, you fiery-footed steeds,
Towards Phoebus' lodging; such a waggoner
As Phaethon would whip you to the west,
And bring in cloudy night immediately.
Spread thy close curtain, love-performing night,
That runaway's eyes may wink, and Romeo
Leap to these arms untalk'd of and unseen!

. . . .

Come, night; come, Romeo; come, thou day in night;
For thou wilt lie upon the wings of night,
Whiter than new snow on a raven's back.
Come, gentle night, come, loving, black-brow'd night.

. . . .

So tedious is this day
As is the night before some festival
To an impatient child that hath new robes
And may not wear them.

The Nurse then enters and increases the effect of haste by maddening the impatient Juliet with confused quibble in reporting Tybalt's death and Romeo's banishment.

It is unnecessary to discuss the full extent to which dispatch appears as a theme in *Romeo and Juliet*. Interpretation need not cover an entire work if it adequately suggests a way of perceiving it. The last half of the play shows a wide range of action, character, and line devoted to the haste theme, but the scenes which carry it most significantly are the ones described below. In no case is extended comment necessary.

Act III, scene iv. This scene of the father and the unsuccessful suitor could readily have been slowed in order to steady the play, but Shakespeare chose to write it in a way which leaves small doubt of his concern, conscious or intuitive, for thematic statement. "So little time" is the note struck from the beginning:

> *Enter* CAPULET, LADY CAPULET, *and* PARIS.
> *Capulet.* Things have fallen out, sir, so unluckily
> That we have had no time to move our daughter.
> Look you, she lov'd her kinsman Tybalt dearly,
> And so did I. Well, we were born to die.
> 'Tis very late, she'll not come down to-night;
> I promise you, but for your company,
> I would have been a-bed an hour ago.
> *Paris.* These times of woe afford no times to woo.
> Madam, good-night; commend me to your daughter.
> *Lady Capulet.* I will, and know her mind early tomorrow;
> To-night she's mewed up to her heaviness.
> *Capulet.* Sir Paris, I will make a desperate tender
> Of my child's love. I think she will be rul'd
> In all respects by me; nay, more, I doubt it not.
> Wife, go you to her ere you go to bed;
> Acquaint her here of my son Paris' love;
> And bid her—mark you me?—on Wednesday next—
> But, soft! what day is this?
> *Paris.*   Monday, my lord.
> *Capulet.* Monday! ha, ha! Well, Wednesday is too soon,
> O' Thursday let it be,—o' Thursday, tell her,
> She shall be married to this noble earl.

Will you be ready? Do you like this haste?
We'll keep no great ado,—a friend or two;
For, hark you, Tybalt being slain so late,
It may be thought we held him carelessly,
Being our kinsman, if we revel much;
Therefore we'll have some half a dozen friends,
And there an end. But what say you to Thursday?
Paris. My lord, I would that Thursday were tomorrow.
Capulet. Well, get you gone; o' Thursday be it, then.
Go you to Juliet ere you go to bed;
Prepare her, wife, against this wedding-day.
Farewell, my lord. Light to my chamber, ho!
Afore me! it is so very late that we
May call it early by and by. Good-night.

Act III, scene v. The elaborate effects of III.iv are repeated here in Lady Capulet's disclosure to Juliet of the plan
for marriage:

Lady Capulet. Well, well, thou hast a careful father, child;
One who, to put thee from thy heaviness,
Hath sorted out a sudden day of joy
That thou expects not nor I look'd not for.
Juliet. Madam, in happy time, what day is that?
Lady Capulet. Marry, my child, early next Thursday morn
The gallant, young, and noble gentleman,
The County Paris, at Saint Peter's Church,
Shall happily make thee there a joyful bride.
Juliet. Now, by Saint Peter's Church and Peter too,
He shall not make me there a joyful bride.
I wonder at this haste that I must wed
Ere he that should be husband comes to woo.

Act IV, scene i. The scene is Friar Laurence's cell. The
issue is again the marriage of Paris and Juliet, and haste
continues as the explicit theme:

Enter FRIAR LAURENCE *and* PARIS.

Friar Laurence. On Thursday, sir? The time is very short.

Paris. My father Capulet will have it so,
And I am nothing slow to slack his haste.

Friar Laurence. You say you do not know the lady's mind.
Uneven is the course, I like it not.

Paris. Immoderately she weeps for Tybalt's death,
And therefore have I little talk'd of love,
For Venus smiles not in a house of tears.
Now, sir, her father counts it dangerous
That she do give her sorrow so much sway,
And in his wisdom hastes our marriage
To stop the inundation of her tears;
Which, too much minded by herself alone,
May be put from her by society.
Now do you know the reason of this haste.

Friar Laurence. [*Aside*] I would I knew not why it should
be slow'd.

Act IV, scene iv. Whether or not the passage quoted
from IV.i sufficiently explains Capulet's hurry, it is quite
apparent three scenes later that he has become preoccupied
with dispatch. At this stage of the play all characters, including the Friar, are stumblers who run fast toward whatever goal they seek.

Enter three of four SERVING-MEN, *with spits,*
logs, and baskets.

Capulet.   Now, fellow,
What's there?

First Servant. Things for the cook, sir; but I know not what.

Capulet. Make haste, make haste. Sirrah, fetch drier logs;
Call Peter, he will show thee where they are.

Second Servant. I have a head, sir, that will find out logs,
And never trouble Peter for the matter.

Capulet. Mass, and well said; a merry whoreson, ha!
Thou shalt be logger-head. Good faith, 'tis day.
The County will be here with music straight,
For so he said he would. I hear him near.
Nurse! Wife! What, ho! What, nurse, I say!
           Re-enter Nurse.
Go waken Juliet, go and trim her up;
I'll go and chat with Paris. Hie, make haste,
Make haste; the bridegroom he is come already.
Make haste, I say.

Also to be found in these lines is the final appearance of a device used throughout the play: servants on the comic level (including the Nurse and Peter) are invariably racing with time. This quirk, of course, is not unusual among stage servants, but the lines which accompany it in *Romeo and Juliet* so forcefully express the haste theme that a far from neutral or conventional effect is produced. The use of a stage convention, moreover, is quite compatible with special effect or meaning.

Finally there is V.iii, the scene at the Capulet tomb which completes the tragedy. Here haste comes to the resting point of death and, to the last, action is accompanied by specific thematic statement. Romeo's dying speech addressed to the Apothecary could have ended with any appropriate sentiment; yet his words are, "Thy drugs are quick," and they are followed by Friar Laurence's entry lines:

Saint Francis be my speed! [2] how oft tonight
Have my old feet stumbled at graves!

[2] "Be my speed" means "prosper me," or "be my protector," but urgency and haste are clearly expressed in this line and the next, which refers to stumbling.

Once more, "they stumble that run fast"—this time over the dead. Juliet's last line aptly echoes Romeo's: "Yea, noise? Then I'll be brief." And the Prince summoned to the scene can speak of tragedy only in terms of the untimely: "What misadventure is so early up . . . ?" He presently calls for delaying time to intervene between the event and its explanation:

> Seal up the mouth of outrage for a while,
> Till we can clear these ambiguities.

It is Friar Laurence who clears them in a summation which slows the precipitous tragedy to a stop. Characteristically, if paradoxically, the Friar begins his long speech on a note of brevity suited to life's hurried span:

> I will be brief, for my short date of breath
> Is not so long as is a tedious tale.

iii. *"Up, cousin, up;*
your heart is up, I know"

IT IS common knowledge that the political theme of *Richard II* [1] symbolized threats to Elizabeth's authority and that the deposition scene was censored in certain editions. The disturbing quality of the play could scarcely have arisen, however, from its explicit doctrine, for in the deposition scene Carlisle proclaims that no subject may judge a king and that, should Bolingbroke be crowned, "The blood of English shall manure the ground,/ And future ages groan for this foul act." Throughout Shakespeare's cycle of history plays this prophecy is recalled at appropriate stages of the epic story. In *Henry V* the King's prayer at the high point of suspense before Agincourt is "Not today, Lord,/ O, not today, think not upon the fault/ My father made in compassing the crown!" This is but one of the allusions in the cycle to the usurpation by Bolingbroke of Richard's throne. The deed was viewed by Elizabethan historians as a kind of secular fall of man which

[1] Although one of the "histories," *Richard II* may be included in a study of Shakespearian tragedy with full propriety under either Elizabethan or modern theory.

tainted generations unborn until England was redeemed from consequent civil war by the Tudor messiah, Henry Earl of Richmond. The doctrine of *Richard II* and the succeeding plays is thus wholly conventional,[2] and the banning of the deposition scene probably occurred not because the play contained objectionable ideas but because the spectacle of usurpation was too disturbing to be presented even with conservative commentary.

It is likely, moreover, that the provocation found in *Richard II* stemmed partly from Shakespeare's vivid characterization. Without authority from the sources, Richard appears as a royal sentimentalist, a defeatist who resigns the throne as though he preferred acting a role of tragedy to one of governing men. And although the sources show Bolingbroke as a victim of extortion who takes over a moribund kingship, Shakespeare magnifies both the extortion and the defunct monarchy. Because of this intensified explanation of Bolingbroke's deed Carlisle's denunciation of the "foul act" of revolution is easy to interpret as a concession to authority, as a piece of stiff morality almost intrusive in Shakespeare's active world of mixed right and wrong. The only difficulty with such an interpretation is that it is too simple. Plainly it rejects the kind of criticism which would find a moral in Carlisle's prophecy alone, but while rejecting one form of simplicity it substitutes another by assuming that complex motivation in drama denies the presence of clear moral judgment.

The political moral of *Richard II* is clear but it is not simple. It can be described adequately only in terms of

[2] I refer to the simplified basic doctrine. To say that this is conventional does not mean that Shakespeare treated simply or conventionally the crises of his characters as they attempt to adhere to the doctrine or depart from it.

the play, which means in part that dramatic structure and development of moral idea are here inseparable. When we understand each in relation to the other, both may appear more effective and more mature than before, and *Richard II* may assume new importance as a landmark in Shakespeare's development as a dramatist.

As resistance against Richard develops at the end of II.i, Northumberland explains the purpose entertained by Bolingbroke's faction:

> If then we shall shake off our slavish yoke,
> Imp out our drooping country's broken wing,
> Redeem from broking pawn the blemished crown,
> Wipe off the dust that hides our sceptre's gilt,
> And make high majesty look like itself. . . .

So far, nothing of deposition; Northumberland's statement is the first of many which stress a goal modestly short of the throne. Two scenes later Bolingbroke's suit is pressed again; the place is Gloucestershire where the insurgent forces encounter old York, regent in Richard's absence. To York's charge of treason "in braving arms against thy sovereign" the reply by Bolingbroke is that he "was banish'd Hereford" but returns "for Lancaster," that he remains a subject of the king, and that having been denied "attorneys" for lawful redress, he has appeared in person. Before Bolingbroke's assembled power which belies his peaceful aims, and before the claim for Henry's inheritance rights, York stands as the strict constructionist:

> My lords of England, let me tell you this;
> I have had feeling of my cousin's wrongs
> And labour'd all I could to do him right;

> But in this kind to come, in braving arms,
> Be his own carver and cut out his way,
> To find out right with wrong—it may not be.

Thus in a scene of unusual strength the rebels are confronted with clear disposition of their pragmatic morality. Ironically, however, in the lines which follow, York collapses pathetically and almost absurdly:

> But if I could, by Him that gave me life,
> I would attach you all and make you stoop
> Unto the sovereign mercy of the king;
> But since I cannot, be it known to you
> I do remain as neuter.

The luxury of neutrality is denied to York, however, through Bolingbroke's request that he accompany the rebels to Bristol in order to "weed and pluck away" Bushy and Bagot, the "caterpillars of the commonwealth." York, the erstwhile absolutist, cannot even decide this incidental issue: "It may be I will go with you; but yet I'll pause,/ For I am loath to break our country's laws." And in any event, "Things past redress are now with me past care."

In the first two scenes of Act III Shakespeare now presents Bolingbroke and Richard in characterization which points to the utter difference in temperament between them; then, having shown each individually in parallel scenes, he brings them together for an episode in which the issue of deposition arises naturally and dramatically from conflict between characters. Dramatic structure, characterization, and presentation of idea (the deposition theme) are fused to the extent that none of these qualities can be discussed properly without reference to the others.

Scene i presents Bolingbroke, and in keeping with the

character it is short and concentrated. It opens in the midst
of events with Henry's terse "Bring forth these men";
Bushy and Green are then presented for his brief but unhurried recitation of the counts against them: they have
misled and "disfigur'd clean" the king; they have "made a
divorce betwixt his queen and him"; they have forced
Bolingbroke to taste "the bitter bread of banishment" and
disinheritance. These deeds condemn them to death. "My
Lord Northumberland, see them dispatch'd." Next, the
queen must be remembered; to York: "Fairly let her be
entreated." And lastly Owen Glendower and his forces must
be met; unhurried orders are so given. In a little over forty
lines Bolingbroke has passed a death sentence, attended to
the amenities of courtesy, and has set a campaign in motion.

Scene ii offers the king and his retinue in a parallel situation, and its contrast with Bolingbroke's scene lies in the
portrayal of Richard first by soliloquies of self-regard, then
by wordy defiance which collapses as he learns of the Welsh
defection, and finally by near hysteria as Aumerle cautions,
"Comfort my liege; remember who you are." When Scroop
enters with worse news, Richard proceeds from the false
stoicism of anticipated defeat to insults directed at his absent
favorites, and back again to sentimental despair:

> Let's choose executors and talk of wills;
> And yet not so; for what can we bequeath
> Save our deposed bodies to the ground?
> Our lands, our lives, and all are Bolingbroke's.

The word "deposed" is repeated as a kind of refrain in the
next few lines as Richard offers to "sit upon the ground/
And tell sad stories of the death of kings." A short speech of
defiance as Carlisle warns against this sitting and wailing of

woes, and a final descent into sentimental resignation as Scroop reports the joining of York with Bolingbroke—these acts complete Richard's performance in the scene. Lest this account of it end as mere description, Shakespeare's inventiveness should be stressed; to the Chronicle version of Richard's misfortune he adds the king's embracing of deposition far in advance of demand or suggestion,[3] and in so doing casts him in a self-made martyr's role. The Flint Castle scene (III.iii) is thus inevitable; figuratively, Richard will depose himself in an agony of play-acting before the unsentimental Bolingbroke.

The outcome at Flint, however, will be unexpected. Not the realist but the sentimentalist will call the turn, and here Shakespeare will answer ironically our question: *when* did Bolingbroke, after all his protests to the contrary, decide to seize the crown? One point of the play, it will appear, is that this question has no point.

In a literal reading, Bolingbroke makes no decision prior to Act IV, and there he is scarcely more than at hand to take the throne. This is subject to several interpretations. First, we might decide that prior to the deposition scene there is no stage at which the deviousness of Bolingbroke becomes clear, and that there are obvious lacunae between his early disclaimers of ambition and his sudden coronation in Act IV. In that event *Richard II* is an inferior play, and the fact that Henry's coronation is also sudden in the

---

[3] See Boswell-Stone, *Shakespere's Holinshed* (London, 1896). Holinshed exhibits Richard in an early state of despair, but with no preconception of dethronement (p. 106), and in a mood of willingness to abdicate after arrival in London (p. 113). Shakespeare, however, presents a king determined to abdicate as early as the landing in Wales (III.ii), before Richard has even encountered Bolingbroke; and he continues to portray him in this mood from there onward.

chronicles does not make it better. Or, secondly, we might conclude that Elizabethan audiences had heard of Boling-broke's wish to be king,[4] and that a dramatist of the time did not need to explain it. This could scarcely be denied, but the play, at least to us, would still be the worse for it. Nor, in spite of occasional statements to the contrary, is it Shakespeare's custom to allow major characterization to rest upon history which is external to the play. A third explanation of our "indecisive" Bolingbroke would be that opportunism, of which he becomes the living symbol, is essentially a tacit vice: that although the opportunist is vaguely aware of the ends to which his means commit him, he relies upon events, not upon declarations, to clarify his purposes. On the basis of the scene at Flint and of two prominent episodes which follow it, I believe that the interpretation just expressed is the one which fits the Henry Bolingbroke of Shakespeare's play.

By the time the Flint scene opens we are aware of Richard's impulses toward virtual abdication, but Boling-broke has never exceeded his demands for simple restitution of rank and estate. Nor have his followers done so. True, York has told him that his very appearance in arms is treason, but Bolingbroke's rejoinder to this has been both disarming and apparently genuine. At the Castle, however, dramatic suggestion begins to take shape. As Henry's followers hold council, Northumberland lets slip the name "Richard" unaccompanied by the title of King. York retorts that such brevity once would have seen him shortened by a

---

[4] Samuel Daniel indicates that in Shakespeare's time Bolingbroke's motives were commonly viewed as suspect. He develops the subject at some length (*Civil Wars*, Book I, stanzas 87–99) and concludes that, in charity, judgment should be suspended.

head's length. Bolingbroke intercedes: "Mistake not, uncle, further than you should." To which York answers: "Take not, cousin, further than you should." This suggestive colloquy is followed by Bolingbroke's characteristic statement of honest intention: "Go to . . . the castle . . . and thus deliver: Henry Bolingbroke/ On both his knees does kiss King Richard's hand/ And sends allegiance and true faith of heart/ To his most royal person." He will lay down his arms if his lands are restored and his banishment repealed. If not, war is the alternative. With dramatic significance, however, Northumberland, who bears this message from a Bolingbroke "on both his knees," fails himself to kneel before Richard and thus becomes again the medium of suggestive disclosure. Richard, in a rage, sends word back to Henry that "ere the crown he looks for live in peace,/ Ten thousand bloody crowns of mothers' sons" shall be the price in slaughter. Northumberland's rejoinder is a yet more pious assertion of Bolingbroke's limited aims: "The King of heaven forbid our lord the King/ Should so with civil and uncivil arms/ Be rush'd upon! Thy thrice noble cousin/ Harry Bolingbroke . . . swears . . . his coming hath no further scope/ Than for his lineal royalties."

Richard's response is to grant the demands, to render a wish in soliloquy that he be buried where his subjects "may hourly trample on their sovereign's head," and, when summoned to the "base court," to make it a further symbol of the rebels' duplicity, to cry out that down, down he comes "like glist'ring Phaethon,/ Wanting the manage of unruly jades." He enters the lowly court, and the scene concludes with a wonderful mummery of sovereignty, each participant speaking as a subject to his king.

Bolingbroke. Stand all apart,
   And show fair duty to His Majesty. [*He kneels down.*]
   My gracious lord—
K. Richard. Fair Cousin, you debase your princely knee
   To make the base earth proud with kissing it.
   Me rather had my heart might feel your love
   Than my unpleas'd eye see your courtesy.
   Up, cousin, up. Your heart is up, I know,
   Thus high at least, although your knee be low.
Bolingbroke. My gracious lord, I come but for mine own.
K. Richard. Your own is yours, and I am yours, and all.
Bolingbroke. So far be mine, my most redoubted lord,
   As my true service shall deserve your love.
K. Richard. Well you deserve. They well deserve to have
   That know the strong'st and surest way to get. . . .
   Cousin, I am too young to be your father,
   Though you are old enough to be my heir.
   What you will have, I'll give, and willing too;
   For do we must what force will have us do.
   Set on toward London, cousin, is it so?
Bolingbroke. Yea, my good lord.
K. Richard. Then I must not say no.

There is no question of what "London" means. It is dethronement for Richard and coronation for Bolingbroke,
an implication which is plain enough here but which Shakespeare underscores in the next scene where the Gardener,
asked by the Queen, "Why dost thou say King Richard is
deposed?" concludes his answer with "Post you to London,
and you will find it so." At Flint, Bolingbroke's reply to
Richard, "Yea, my good lord," is the aptly timed climax
of the episode, and of the play. With this oblique admission,
coming with great effect immediately after his statement
of loyalty and subjection, Henry's purposes become clear,
and the significant fact is that not he but Richard has phrased

his intent. The king's single line, "Set on toward London, cousin, is it so?" is the ironic instrument for exposing a long course of equivocation which the rebels seem to have concealed even from themselves.[5] And in fact Bolingbroke is still trying to conceal it; his short answer is the minimum assertion of his motives, an opportunist's spurious appeal to what "must be" in order to avoid a statement of purpose.

This turn in the play rests upon skillful fusion of three elements—plot construction, disclosure of political moral, and characterization, all of which show parallel irony. In plot unfoldment, the end of the Flint scene is the point of climax at which Henry's true purpose is revealed. But the climax is also a studied anticlimax, for the rebels advance upon Flint Castle only, as it were, to find it abandoned and with the words, "Come to London," written upon the walls. They, and the audience, had expected not quiet exposure of their aims (the actual climax) but dramatic opportunity for constitutional manifestoes.

As for disclosure of political doctrine, it is during the encounter at Flint that the rebels achieve their most eloquent statement of legality in seeking only a subject's claim to justice from his king. But the luxury of that pretense vanishes at the end of the scene, again with the word "London."

---

[5] Self-delusion on Bolingbroke's part is a trait clearly suggested by Daniel in his enigmatic passage on Henry's motives (*Civil Wars*, Book I, stanzas 90–91). I mention this only to show that such an interpretation was made at the time *Richard II* was written. The concluding lines of stanza 91 are:

Men do not know what then themselves will be
When-as, more than themselves, themselves they see.

For an additional reference to Daniel, as well as for a denial that Bolingbroke is a conscious schemer, see J. Dover Wilson's edition of *Richard II* (Cambridge, 1939), pp. xx and xxi. Mr. Wilson briefly describes Bolingbroke as an opportunist led by Fortune.

It becomes suddenly apparent that York's previous judgment was sound, that Bolingbroke's use of force to gain
just concessions from his sovereign has committed him
to the destruction of sovereignty.

The third factor here is characterization which greatly
enhances the complex of ironies. Shakespeare's prior es-
tablishment of Bolingbroke's realism, self-containment, and
resourcefulness, along with Richard's romantic defeatism,
near-hysteria, and pathetic reliance upon others, has furnished a decided pattern for the meeting of the two at
Flint. Bolingbroke (with Northumberland) fulfills previously set notes of stability and restraint; Richard repeats
the performance he had enacted before his own followers in
the preceding scene, and reminds us of a familiar epigram
about the protagonist who is spectator at his own tragedy.
Full portraiture of Bolingbroke and Richard, both before
and during the Castle episode, thus prepares for the para-
doxical ending of the scene. There, with Richard's knowing reference to London and Bolingbroke's one-line reply,
the shift in characterization materializes. The unstable
Richard, who had fled from facts through every form of
emotional exaggeration, now drops his sentimental role
and points to reality with quiet wit and candor; the plain-
dealing Bolingbroke who had offered his demands with
such consistency and seeming honesty, now admits his sham
of rebellion which was to stop short of rebellion.

The end of Act III, scene iii, is thus pivotal. At this point
of multiple effect Bolingbroke's ambiguity is revealed, and
it now engages Shakespeare's attention in a pair of episodes
which will complete Henry's portrait; the ambiguity will be

presented twice again by means of the same dramatic method.

The first of these cumulative parallels to the Flint scene occurs in IV.i (the deposition). Here Richard is again confronted by the rebels, and again he is by turns both defiant and submissive; his sentimental display is likewise in dramatic contrast with Henry's simplicity, forbearance, and directness. And as before, the paradox comes in the closing lines:

> *K. Richard.* I'll beg one boon,
> And then be gone and trouble you no more.
> Shall I obtain it?
> *Bolingbroke.* Name it, fair Cousin.
> *K. Richard.* "Fair Cousin"? I am greater than a king.
> For when I was a king, my flatterers
> Were then but subjects. Being now a subject,
> I have a King here to my flatterer.
> Being so great, I have no need to beg.
> *Bolingbroke.* Yet ask.
> *K. Richard.* And shall I have?
> *Bolingbroke.* You shall.
> *K. Richard.* Then give me leave to go.
> *Bolingbroke.* Whither?
> *K. Richard.* Whither you will, so I were from your sights.
> *Bolingbroke.* Go, some of you convey him to the Tower.

Just as "London" meant deposition at the end of III.iii, so here at the end of IV.i the Tower means imprisonment and ultimate death. Again Richard, who has run his course of theatrical emotion, becomes pointedly realistic; again Bolingbroke, who has exhibited every sign of gracious honesty, reveals duplicity in a concluding line.

The third and final step in Henry's portrayal is analogous in all essentials to the two scenes we have examined. The

fact that Shakespeare here drew upon the Chronicles might
imply that he found there a suggestion of the shifting taciturnity which Bolingbroke shows in all three episodes. Piers
of Exton, in V.iv, ponders something he has heard. "Have I
no friend will rid me of this living fear?" Was not that what
the new king said? And did he not repeat it as he "wishtly
look'd on me"? It is enough; Exton promptly murders
Richard and returns with the body. Henry's lines which
conclude the play are well known; he admits desiring
Richard's death but disowns Exton's act and pledges expiation in a voyage to the Holy Land.

Three times—at the end of III.iii, at the end of the deposition scene, and in the Exton scenes at the end of the play—
Henry has taken, if it may be so called, a decisive step. Each
time the move he has made has been embodied in a terse statement, and each time someone else has either evoked it from
him or stated its implications for him. Never in sixteenth-
century drama were motives disclosed with such economy
and understatement. The Elizabethan stage character with a
moral contradiction usually explains his flaw before, during,
and after the event—and at length. Until the short choric
"confession" at the very end of the play, Bolingbroke, however, shows his deviousness in one-line admissions spaced
at telling intervals and occurring in contexts which are
effectively similar.

And as each of these admissions marks a step in characterization, it indicates a critical stage of plot development:
the conflict of forces is resolved with the line on London
concluding the Flint Castle scene, for there Richard and
Henry reach mutual understanding on the dethronement
issue; the falling action becomes defined with the line near

the end of the deposition scene which sends Richard to the Tower; the catastrophe is begun by the line to Exton which sends him to death.

Finally, at each of these three points the meaning implicit in the play shows a new clarity. With the reference to London at Flint it becomes apparent that a "constitutional" show of force against sovereignty leads to the deposition of sovereignty; with the dispatching of Richard to the Tower it appears that deposition of sovereignty requires degradation of the sovereign; and with Henry's line to Exton it becomes plain that murder of sovereignty must be the final outcome.[6]

From his first history to his last tragedy Shakespeare excelled in a poet's expression of Tudor political dogma. But to say this is not enough, for as early as *Richard II* he combined his poet's talent with another difficult art. In this play doctrine, plot, and characterization unfold integrally. With our debt to the English and American revolutions we cannot admire the doctrine, but we can recognize in *Richard II* a stage of Shakespeare's development at which morality and artistry become functionally inseparable.

[6] The Chronicle accounts of Richard's latter days do not provide a suggestion of these cumulative steps. As usual, a play-source comparison emphasizes Shakespeare's artistry both in structure and motivation. Daniel (*Civil Wars*, Books I and II) likewise fails to present Bolingbroke's opportunistic conduct in the telling manner of Shakespeare. He does amply suggest the possibility of "unconscious" drift toward usurpation but in no way dramatizes this action in successive, cumulative disclosure. Daniel is not to be regarded with certainty as a source of Shakespeare; it is possible that similarities between the *Civil Wars* and *Richard II* are to be accounted for by Daniel having seen the play. In any event, a comparison of Shakespeare and Daniel is revealing.

iv. *"Or else were this a savage spectacle"*

MODERN readers are prone to find the tragedy of Brutus in his rigid devotion to justice and fair play. Many members of the Globe audience, however, believed that his virtues were complicated by self-deception and doubtful principle. In sixteenth-century views of history the conspiracy against Caesar often represented a flouting of unitary sovereignty, that prime point of Tudor policy, and exemplified the anarchy thought to accompany "democratic" or constitutional checks upon authority. Certain judgments of Elizabethan political writers who refer to Brutus are quite clear upon this point.[1] Although naturally aware of his disinterested honor and liberality, contem-

[1] See the discussion in J. E. Phillips's *The State in Shakespeare's Greek and Roman Plays* (New York, 1940), pp. 172 ff. Mr. Phillips quotes at length from such typical spokesmen as Sir Thomas Elyot and Thomas Craig. His analysis of *Julius Caesar* on this basis is also illuminating. See also the present author's *The Populace in Shakespeare* (New York, 1949), p. 147, for a condemnation by William Covell of Romans who aroused civil dissension by covering their purposes "with the fine terms of a common good, of the freedom of the people, of justice. . . ." The parallel with Brutus is a very close one, and Covell, moreover, explicitly avows a topical relation of such Roman history to the civil tensions of Elizabethan England.

porary audiences could thus perceive in him a conflict between questionable goals and honorable action, a contradiction lying in his attempt to redeem morally confused ends
by morally clarified means. The Elizabethan tragedy of
Brutus, like that of Othello, is marked by an integrity of
conduct which leads the protagonist into evil and reassures
him in his error.

The distinction between modern and Elizabethan views
of *Julius Caesar* is not the point of our inquiry, but it is a
necessary beginning, for the older view of Brutus determines
both the symbolic quality and the structure of the play. I
hope to show that a sixteenth-century idea of Brutus is as
thoroughly related to Shakespeare's art as it is to his meaning.

When a dramatist wishes to present an idea, his traditional
method, of course, is to settle upon an episode in which the
idea arises naturally but vividly from action and situation.
Such an episode in *Julius Caesar* is the one in which Brutus
resolves to exalt not only the mission but the tactics of conspiracy: having accepted republicanism as an honorable
end, he sets out to dignify assassination, the means, by lifting
it to a level of rite and ceremony.[2] In II.i, as Cassius urges
the killing of Antony as a necessary accompaniment to the
death of Caesar, Brutus declares that "such a course will
seem too bloody . . . ,/ To cut the head off and then hack
the limbs." With this thought a sense of purpose comes over
him: "Let's be sacrificers, but not butchers, Caius." Here
his conflict seems to be resolved, and for the first time he is

[2] My article on the ritual theme in *Julius Caesar* (*PMLA*, LXVI,
765 ff.) appeared in 1951 as an early draft of this chapter. Some of my
principal observations have been repeated by Ernest Schanzer in a
recent essay ("The Tragedy of Shakespeare's Brutus," *ELH*, March,
1955, pp. 1 ff.; see pp. 6–8).

more than a reluctant presence among the conspirators as he expands the theme which ends his hesitation and frees his moral imagination:

> We all stand up against the spirit of Caesar,
> And in the spirit of men there is no blood;
> Oh, that we then could come by Caesar's spirit,
> And not dismember Caesar! But, alas,
> Caesar must bleed for it! And, gentle friends,
> Let's kill him boldly, but not wrathfully;
> Let's carve him as a dish fit for the gods,
> Not hew him as a carcass fit for hounds.

This proposed conversion of bloodshed to ritual is the manner in which an abstract Brutus will be presented in terms of concrete art. From the suggestion of Plutarch that Brutus' first error lay in sparing Antony, Shakespeare moves to the image of Antony as a limb of Caesar, a limb not to be hacked because hacking is no part of ceremonial sacrifice. From Plutarch's description of Brutus as high-minded, gentle and disinterested, Shakespeare proceeds to the Brutus of symbolic action. Gentleness and disinterestedness become embodied in the act of "unwrathful" blood sacrifice. High-mindedness becomes objectified in ceremonial observance.

A skeptical reader may ask why the episode just described is any more significant than a number of others such as Brutus' scene with Portia or his quarrel with Cassius. If more significant, it is so only because of its relation to a thematic design. I agree, moreover, that Shakespeare gains his effects by variety; as a recognition, in fact, of his complexity I hope to show that the structure of *Julius Caesar* is marked by reference both varied and apt to Brutus' sacrificial rite, and that this process includes expository preparation in earlier scenes, emphasis upon "mock-ceremony" in both earlier and later scenes, and repeated comment by Antony upon butchery under the guise of sacrifice—ironical comment which takes final form in the parley before Philippi.

Derived in large measure from Plutarch, but never mechanically or unselectively, the theme of incantation and ritual is thus prominent throughout *Julius Caesar,* and this is no less true at the beginning than during the crucial episodes of Acts II and III. In the opening scene of the play we are confronted with a Roman populace rebuked by Marullus for ceremonial idolatry of Caesar:

> And do you now put on your best attire?
> And do you now cull out a holiday?
> And do you now strew flowers in his way
> That comes in triumph over Pompey's blood?

For this transgression Marullus prescribes a counter-observance by the citizens in immediate expiation of their folly:

> Run to your houses, fall upon your knees,
> Pray to the gods to intermit this plague
> That needs must light on this ingratitude.

To which Flavius adds:

> Go, go, good countrymen, and for this fault,
> Assemble all the poor men of your sort;
> Draw them to Tiber banks, and weep your tears
> Into the channel, till the lowest stream
> Do kiss the most exalted shores of all.

And after committing the populace to these rites of atonement for their festal celebration of Caesar, the two tribunes themselves leave to remove the devotional symbols set up for his welcoming. "Go you . . . towards the Capitol;/ This way will I. Disrobe the images/ If you do find them decked with ceremonies./ . . . let no images/ Be hung with Caesar's trophies." It is the hope of Flavius that these dis-enchantments will make Caesar "fly an ordinary pitch,/ Who else would soar above the view of men."

Act I, scene ii is equally unusual in carrying the theme of ritual. It is apparent that Shakespeare had a wide choice of means for staging the entry of Caesar and his retinue; yet he selects an entry based upon Plutarch's description of the "feast Lupercalia" in which the rite of touching or striking barren women by runners of the course is made prominent. Caesar, moreover, after ordering Calpurnia to be so touched by Antony, commands: "Set on; and leave no ceremony out." It can be said, in fact, that the whole of this scene is written with ceremonial observance as a background. Its beginning, already described, is followed by a touch of solemnity in the soothsayer's words; next comes its main expository function, the sounding of Brutus by Cassius, and throughout this interchange come at intervals the shouts and flourishes of a symbolic spectacle. When the scene is again varied by formal reentry and exit of Caesar's train, Casca remains behind to make a mockery of the rite which has loomed so large from off-stage. Significantly, in Casca's travesty of the ceremonial crown-offering and of the token offering by Caesar of his throat for cutting, Shakespeare has added a satirical note which does not appear in Plutarch.

The process, then, in each of the two opening episodes has been the bringing of serious ritual into great prominence, and of subjecting it to satirical treatment. In the first scene the tribunes denounce the punctilio planned for Caesar's entry, send the idolatrous crowd to rites of purification, and set off themselves to desecrate the devotional images. In the second scene a multiple emphasis of ceremony is capped by Casca's satire which twists the crown ritual into imbecile mummery. At this point, and in conformity with the mood set by Casca, occurs Cassius' mockery in soliloquy of Brutus:

> Well, Brutus, thou art noble; yet I see
> Thy honorable mettle may be wrought
> From that it is dispos'd; therefore it is meet
> That noble minds keep ever with their likes;
> For who is so firm that cannot be seduc'd?

The next scene (I.iii) is packed with omens and supernatural portents, a note which is carried directly into II.i where Brutus, on receiving the mysterious papers which have been left to prompt his action, remarks,

> The exhalations whizzing in the air
> Give so much light that I may read by them.

Appropriately, the letters read under this weird glow evoke his first real commitment to the "cause":

> O Rome, I make thee promise,
> If the redress will follow, thou receivest
> Thy full petition at the hand of Brutus!

Now appear his lines on the interim "between the acting of a dreadful thing/ And the first motion" in which "the state of man/ Like to a little kingdom, suffers then/ The nature of a insurrection." This conventional symbolizing of political convulsion by inward insurrection is followed by the soliloquy on conspiracy:

O, then by day
Where wilt thou find a cavern dark enough
To mask thy monstrous visage? Seek none, Conspiracy!
Hide it in smiles and affability.

The conflict within Brutus thus becomes clear in this scene. First, the participant in revolution suffers revolution within himself; then the hater of conspiracy and lover of plain dealing must call upon Conspiracy to hide in smiling courtesy.

We have now reached the critical point (II.i.154 ff.) to which attention was first called, an outward presentation of Brutus' crisis through his acceptance of an assassin's role upon condition that the assassins become sacrificers. Already a theme well established in preceding scenes, the idea of ritual is again made prominent. As the soliloquy on conspiracy closes, the plotters gather, and the issue becomes the taking of an oath. Brutus rejects this as an idle ceremony unsuited to men joined in the honesty of a cause and turns now to the prospect of Caesar's death. This time, however, honorable men do need ceremony, ceremony which will purify the violent act of all taint of butchery and raise it to the level of sacrifice. But although Brutus has steadied himself with a formula his conflict is still unresolved, for as he sets his course he "unconsciously" reveals the evasion which Antony later will amplify: to transmute political killing into ritual is to cloak it with appearances. We began with Brutus' passage on carving Caesar as a dish for the gods; these are the lines which complete it:

And let our hearts, as subtle masters do,
Stir up their servants to an act of rage,
And after seem to chide 'em. This shall make

> Our purpose necessary and not envious;
> Which so appearing to the common eyes,
> We shall be called purgers, not murderers.

The contradiction is interesting. In an anticlimax, Brutus has ended his great invocation to ritual with a note on practical politics: our hearts shall stir us and afterward seem to chide us; we shall thus "appear" to the citizenry as purgers, not murderers.

Shakespeare never presents Brutus as a demagogue, but there are ironical traces of the politician in him which suggest Covell's adverse picture of Roman liberators.[3] It is curious, in fact, that although Brutus is commonly thought to be unconcerned over public favor, he expresses clear concern for it in the passage just quoted and in III.i.244–251, where he sanctions Antony's funeral speech only if Antony agrees to tell the crowd that he speaks by generous permission, and only if he agrees to utter no evil of the conspiracy. Nor is Brutus' speech in the Forum wholly the non-political performance it is supposed to be; certainly Shakespeare's Roman citizens are the best judges of it, and they react tempestuously. Although compressed, it scarcely discloses aloofness or an avoidance of popular emotive themes.

Act II, scene ii now shifts to the house of Caesar, but the emphasis on ritual continues as before. With dramatic irony, in view of Brutus' recent lines on sacrificial murder, Caesar commands, "Go bid the priests do present sacrifice." Calpurnia who has "never stood on ceremonies" (omens) is now terrified by them. News comes that the augurers, plucking the entrails of an offering, have failed to find a heart. Calpurnia has dreamed that smiling Romans have laved their

---

[3] See the reference and quotation in note 1, p. 40.

hands in blood running from Caesar's statue, and Decius Brutus gives this its favorable interpretation which sends Caesar to his death.

The vivid assassination scene carries out Brutus' ritual prescription in dramatic detail, for the killing is staged with a formalized approach, ending in kneeling, by one conspirator after another until the victim is surrounded. This is met by a series of retorts from Caesar ending in "Hence! Wilt thou lift up Olympus," and the "sacrifice" is climaxed with his "Et tu Brute!" The conspirators ceremonially bathe their hands in Caesar's blood, and Brutus pronounces upon "this our lofty scene" with the prophecy that it "shall be acted over/ In states unborn and accents yet unknown!"

The mockery in counterritual now begins as a servant of Antony enters (III.i.121) and confronts Brutus:

> Thus, Brutus, did my master bid me kneel,
> Thus did Mark Antony bid me fall down;
> And being prostrate, thus he bade me say:
> Brutus is noble, wise, valiant, and honest.

Here a threefold repetition, "kneel," "fall down," and "being prostrate," brings the ceremonial irony close to satire. Following this worship of the new idol by his messenger, Antony appears in person and with dramatic timing offers himself as a victim. In one speech he evokes both the holy scene which the conspirators so desired and the savagery which underlay it:

> Now, whilst your purpled hands do reek and smoke,
> Fulfill your pleasure. Live a thousand years,
> I shall not find myself so apt to die;
> No place will please me so, no mean of death,
> As here by Caesar, and by you cut off.

The murder scene is thus hallowed by Antony in a manner
which quite reverses its sanctification by the conspirators.
Brutus, forbearing, attempts to mollify Antony with his
cherished theme of purgation:

> Our hearts you see not. They are pitiful,
> And pity to the general wrong of Rome—
> As fire drives out fire, so pity pity—
> Hath done this deed on Caesar.

Antony's response is again one of counterceremony, the
shaking of hands in formal sequence which serves to make
each conspirator stand alone and unprotected by the rite of
blood which had united him with the others. The assassins
had agreed as a token of solidarity that each of them should
stab Caesar. Antony seems to allude to this:

> Let each man render me his bloody hand.
> First, Marcus Brutus, will I shake with you;
> Now, Caius Cassius, do I take your hand;
> Now, Decius Brutus, yours; now yours, Mettellus;
> Yours, Cinna; and, my valiant Casca, yours;
> Though last, not least in love, yours, good Trebonius.
> Gentlemen all,—alas what shall I say?

It is then that Antony, addressing the body of Caesar, suddenly delivers his first profanation of the ritual sacrifice:

> Here wast thou bay'd brave hart;
> Here didst thou fall; and here thy hunters stand,
> Sign'd in thy spoil, and crimson'd in thy lethe.

And lest the allusion escape, Shakespeare continues Antony's
inversion of Brutus' ceremonial formula: the dish carved for
the gods is doubly transformed into the carcass hewn for
hounds with further hunting metaphors of Caesar as a hart
in the forest and as "a deer strucken by many princes,"

Brutus agrees to give reasons why Caesar was dangerous, "or else were this a savage spectacle," and the stage is set for what may be called the play's chief counterritual. Only Brutus, who planned the rite of sacrifice, could with such apt irony arrange the "true rites" and "ceremonies" which are to doom the conspiracy.

> I will myself into the pulpit first
> And show the reason of our Caesar's death.
> What Antony shall speak, I will protest
> He speaks by leave and by permission,
> And that we are contented Caesar shall
> Have all true rites and lawful ceremonies.

But exactly after the manner of his speech announcing the ritual sacrifice (II.i) Brutus concludes again on a note of policy: "It shall advantage more than do us wrong."

Next follows Antony *solus* rendering his prophecy of "domestic fury and fierce civil strife" symbolized in Caesar's ghost which will

> Cry "Havoc," and let slip the dogs of war,
> That this foul deed shall smell above the earth.

The passage is similar in utterance, function, and dramatic placement to Carlisle's prophecy on the deposition of Richard II, and for that reason it is to be taken seriously as a choric interpretation of Caesar's death. Significantly, the beginning lines again deride Brutus' erstwhile phrase, "sacrificers but not butchers":

> O, pardon me, thou bleeding piece of earth,
> That I am meek and gentle with these butchers!

It is unnecessary to elaborate upon the Forum scene; Antony's oration follows the speech of Brutus with consequences familiar to all readers. But there is an element in Antony's turning of the tables which is just as remarkable as the well-known irony of his references to "honorable men." If we remember that Shakespeare has emphasized ritual at various planes of seriousness and of derision, the conclusion of Antony's speech to the populace will link itself with the previous theme. For here Antony reenacts the death of Caesar in a ritual of his own, one intended to show that the original "lofty scene" presented a base carnage. Holding Caesar's bloody mantle as a talisman, he reproduces *seriatim* the sacrificial strokes, but he does so in terms of the "rent" Casca made and the "cursed steel" that Brutus plucked away with the blood of Caesar following it. Again, each conspirator had struck individually at Caesar and had symbolically involved himself with the others; for the second time Antony reminds us of this ritual bond by recounting each stroke, and his recreation of the rite becomes a mockery of it. Brutus' transformation of blood into the heady wine of sacrifice is reversed both in substance and in ceremony.

For the "realists" among the conspirators what has occurred can be summed up in the bare action of the play: the killing of Caesar has been accomplished, but the fruits of it have been spoiled by Brutus' insistence that Antony live and that he speak at Caesar's funeral. "The which," as North's Plutarch has it, "marred all." With reference to Brutus, however, something much more significant has been enacted; the "insurrection," the contradiction, within him has taken outward form in his attempt to purify assassination through ceremony. This act, not to be found in Plutarch,[4] symbolizes the "Elizabethan" Brutus compelled by honor to join with conspirators but required by conscience to reject Conspiracy.

We have followed the ritual theme in *Julius Caesar* from early scenes to the point of Antony's oration, at which it is completely defined. There remains, however, a terminal appearance of the theme in the first scene of Act V. The ultimate clash between the idealism of Brutus and Antony's contempt for it comes during the parley on the eve of

[4] A reference at this point to Plutarch will serve both to clarify my meaning and to allay some natural doubts concerning the dramatist's intention. While it is true that the ritual murder of Caesar is Shakespeare's own contribution, the expository preparation for it in Act I comes from an episode in Plutarch in which Antony concludes the Lupercalian rites by offering a laurel crown twice to Caesar, and in which the tribunes are described as desecrating ritual offerings (*Shakespeare's Plutarch*, I, 92–93; see also II, 19–20). Hence we have basic ritual materials for Shakespeare's first two scenes present in one convenient block of his source which also offered a convenient beginning for the play. Does this prevent us from attaching significance to the unusual presence of ritual elements in the exposition scenes? I believe it does not, for two reasons. First, the choice of source material by a dramatist is itself significant; Shakespeare could have started the play with other episodes in Plutarch or with scenes of his own invention. Secondly, it is immaterial whether he began *Julius Caesar* with this episode in his source and, because of its wealth of ritual detail, was led to the theme of ritualized assassination, or whether he began with the theme and chose source materials for exposition which agreed with it. In either case the same remarkable unity between earlier and later parts of the play would have been achieved, and it is this unity which is important. Guesses about its origin in the playwright's composition are profitless. We do know that Shakespeare's Brutus plans the killing of Caesar as ritual, while Plutarch presents it as the very opposite of this. Plutarch's description of the assassination emphasizes, in fact, its resemblance to the hunting down of an animal, the very effect Brutus seeks explicitly to avoid in the "carcass-hounds" figure, and the one which Antony magnifies in his counteremphasis of imagery drawn from hunting. North notes it thus: "Caesar turned him nowhere but he was stricken at by some . . . and was hacked and mangled among them, as a wild beast taken of hunters." (*Shakespeare's Plutarch*, I, 101–2.)

Philippi, at which Antony again drives home the old issue of ceremonial imposture. Brutus has observed that his enemy wisely threats before he stings; the reply is Antony's last disposition of the sacrificial rite:

> Villains, you did not so when your vile daggers
> Hack'd one another in the sides of Caesar,
> You show'd your teeth like apes, and fawn'd like
>   hounds,
> And bow'd like bondmen, kissing Caesar's feet;
> Whilst damned Casca, like a cur, behind
> Struck Caesar on the neck.

Antony invokes the "hacking" which Brutus earlier fore-swore, and he again inverts the cherished formula of sacrifice: once more the dish carved for gods becomes the carcass hewn for hounds. Over the body of Caesar he had previously employed the hunting-hound figure ("Here wast thou bay'd, brave hart."); the apes, the hounds, and the cur of these lines complete his vengeful irony of metaphor.

What, finally, is to be inferred from Antony's concluding passage on "the noblest Roman of them all"? Commonly found there is a broad vindication of Brutus which would deny an ironical interpretation. When Antony's elegiac speech is read plainly, however, its meaning is quite limited: it declares simply that Brutus was the only conspirator un-touched by envy, and that, in intention, he acted "in a general honest thought/ And common good to all." The Elizabethan view of Brutus as tragically misguided is thus consistent with Antony's pronouncement that he was the only disinterested member of the conspiracy. But Brutus is not to be summed up in an epitaph; as the impersonal member of a conspiracy motivated largely by personal ends, he sought in a complex way to resolve his contradiction by de-personalizing, ritualizing, the means.

Shakespeare's achievement, however, is not confined to the characterization of a major figure, for we have seen that the ceremonial motive extends beyond the personality of Brutus into the structure of the play. Exposition stressing the idea of ritual observance leads to the episode in which Brutus formulates the "sacrifice," and clear resolution of the idea follows in event and commentary. Structural crafts-manship thus supplements characterization and the two combine, as in *Richard II*, to state the political philosophy implicit in the play.

v. "Give me that man
that is not passion's slave"

AS the Olivier motion picture *Hamlet* opens, a disembodied voice is heard to say, "This is a play about a man who could not make up his mind." These words are doubly strange when we recall that Mr. Olivier cut many of the lines upon which the Hamlet of pale thought has traditionally rested. Thus has the Coleridge Hamlet become a mythic being who must be placated before maimed rites of a quite un-Coleridgean nature are performed; thus has the production of *Hamlet* become a ceremony which denies the incantation that begins it.

The fault was hardly Mr. Olivier's. His difficulty arose from a conflict between the enduring Coleridge tradition and the recognized difficulty of expressing Coleridge's Hamlet through the action of Shakespeare's play. It is now scarcely possible to look upon the feigned madness, or upon the elaborately contrived mousetrap, or upon the refusal to kill Claudius at prayer, as external results of thinking too precisely on the event. But this does not mean that the problem has been simplified, for the historical scholarship which finds a robust Hamlet in the action often admits a quite contrary character in the soliloquies. Such interpretation began early and has itself formed a tradition. Many years ago C. M. Lewis reasoned that Hamlet's refinements of inner conflict were superimposed upon a primitive inherited plot,[1] and little extension of this theory is needed to produce a character who acts with simple dispatch but who dwells upon his complex inability to do so. Had Eliot [2] sensed this larger difficulty instead of the rather questionable one suggested by his reading of Robertson, he might have found even less of an "objective correlative" for Hamlet's thoughts and emotions.

A usual way out of such dualism is to reflect that Shakespeare throve on inconsistency and to look upon *Hamlet* as a great play but a failure in coherence. But it is assumed, I trust, that this view should be entertained only if the facts require it. Is there, after all, a character interpretation which fits both the soliloquies and the action? Is there a central theme which unites character, plot, subplot, and allegedly digressive features such as the player scenes? Does such a theme arise from dramatic emphasis apparent to a mature spectator, whether Elizabethan or modern?

In attempting to answer these questions I shall try to show that Hamlet's conflict is one in which a sense of underemotion leads to overemotion, and in which guilt accompanies either state of feeling. Whatever may be said of this interpretation, it leads to no inconsistency between Hamlet's Shakespearian thoughts and his deeds inherited from the pre-Shakespearian plot. A Hamlet who acts supremely but who is unable to accompany action with suit-

[1] *The Genesis of* Hamlet (New York, 1907).
[2] "Hamlet" (1919), in *Selected Essays* (New York, 1950), pp. 121-26.

able feeling will present none of the confusion caused by a Hamlet who acts efficiently but who cannot, for various reasons, face the world of action.

To state that Hamlet's difficulty is one of passion rather than of will is to advance nothing disturbing or anachronistic, nor above all, is it to deny that his mind remains the most interesting side of his personality. Miss Campbell has long since given her view of Hamlet as a "slave of passion," and Mr. G. Wilson Knight has also observed some elements from which my interpretation proceeds.[3] The historical view of the character which I shall offer is one that finds Shakespeare adapting the old plot but providing complex characterization which is quite consistent with it. Characterization, however, will not be our main problem; we shall be concerned with a psychological interpretation, but this will contribute to a view of the play as a whole in which a theme, emotive deficiency and excess, controls the main plot, the subplot, the soliloquies, and the player episodes. This theme, moreover, evolves cumulatively from the beginning of the play to its ironical climax in the grave scene.

In Act I, scene ii the theme is quickly established. Claudius and the queen present Hamlet's "unmanly grief" for his father as an excess of sensibility, and while their conception of him is a false one, it plainly introduces the note of emotional balance or decorum. The stage is now cleared for the first soliloquy which is Hamlet's own projection of the theme: his familiar avowal that the world's "uses" seem

[3] Lily B. Campbell, *Shakespeare's Tragic Heroes: Slaves of Passion* (Cambridge, 1930; New York, 1952). Miss Campbell's interpretation of *Hamlet* does not, of course, resemble mine. I shall refer to Mr. Knight's contribution in observations and notes which follow.

"weary, stale, flat, and unprofitable." From this state of barren emotion he proceeds, after the manner of later scenes into great emotional intensity and in so doing assails Gertrude's waning remembrance of his father—precisely the fault he will later find in himself.

The Polonius-Laertes subplot is introduced in the next scene; the theme, however, continues on a secondary level. Ophelia is warned of Hamlet's impulsive ardor, "a toy in blood,/ A violet in the youth of primy nature,/ Forward, not permanent, sweet, not lasting." This need not be taken literally as characterization, but it deserves recognition as a restatement of theme. Laertes, moreover, warns Ophelia: "And keep within the rear of your affection." All of this advice is expanded by Polonius in turn, but only after he has delivered the well-known lines to his son which express the theme on still another secondary level. Every deft platitude, save the borrower-lender one, specifies an ideal of balance in emotion leading to decorum in action.

Hamlet encounters the ghost (I.v.) in a scene which can be called the climax of Act I. His first affective response is one of dedication; he will "wipe away all trivial, fond records,/ . . . all pressures past," that the ghost's command "alone shall live" in his consciousness. This, however, is immediately succeeded by an episode in which for the first time we hear the Hamlet of "wild and whirling words." The scene ends, however, on a note of decisiveness as the watchers are sworn by Hamlet to serve his ends. Thus has the staleness and flatness of I.ii, given way to concentration of feeling. At II.ii.304 ff., however, Hamlet renews the mood of I.ii as he declares to Rosencrantz and Guildenstern that he has lost his mirth, "foregone all custom of exercise"; "in-

deed, it goes so heavily with my disposition that this goodly
frame, the earth, seems to me a sterile promontory."

Lines 453 ff. of II.ii present a phase of the player-scene in
which there are skilled and lively variations upon the already established theme, so that the colloquy with the actors
avoids the usual charge of topical digression. Again, the note
is affective balance and soundness. Hamlet remembers "an
excellent play, well digested in the scenes, set down with as
much modesty as cunning." There was "no matter in the
phrase that might indict the author of affectation," and the
composition showed "an honest method, as wholesome as
sweet." After such praise of controlled feeling on the plane
of artistry, Hamlet now recites bombastic lines from this
"modest" play which, in their departure from his description, reveal the unstable relation between his ideal of emotive balance and his indulgence in emotive extremes. One
may object, of course, that the rhetorical excess is merely
intended to satirize outmoded playwriting or to distinguish
play-within-play from the play itself. As literary historians
we should recognize, however, that dramatists often have
plural motives, and that there is no reason why Hamlet's
affinity here for the rhetoric of passion cannot have a function beyond the mechanical ones favored by skeptical tradition.

After the First Player has picked up the passage and carried it over the brink of passion, Hamlet turns the implied
theme into direct expression with the "rogue and peasant
slave" soliloquy. What would this player do—the player
with "tears in his eyes, distraction in's aspect,/ A broken
voice"—what would he do "had he the motive and the cue
for passion/ That I have?" Yet Hamlet, dull and muddy

mettled, peaks like John-a-Dreams, unpregnant of his cause.
Self-shamed by inadequacy of feeling, he proceeds into the
"bloody, bawdy villain" lines; then doubly shamed by hysteria which is worse than no feeling at all, he compares himself to a cursing drab, a whore, for unpacking his heart with
words. At which he veers again, this time toward the plane
of balanced action: "The play's the thing."

Mr. Knight comments upon Hamlet's sense of emotional
inferiority in this episode, and notes briefly the scene's resemblance to the grave scene; he then observes that what
Hamlet wants "is something more than curses and less . . .
than bloodshed." [4] I suggest, however, that what he wants
here is something less than curses and more than emotional
dullness. In any case, he never shrinks from the idea of violent revenge—"Now could I drink hot blood . . ."

So instead of topical digression in the elaborate scene with
the players in II.ii, there is a heightened repetition of the
pattern found in the opening action. In Act I the order is
thus: Hamlet's "weary, stale" state (I.ii), the ideal of balanced emotion expressed through the subplot (I.iii), Hamlet's emotional disturbance (I.v), and finally his decision
on the antic disposition. In II.ii, after line 304, there is the
directly parallel but accelerated sequence: Hamlet's "sterile"
mood (the scene with Rosencrantz and Guildenstern), his

---

[4] *The Wheel of Fire* (4th ed.; London, 1949; reprinted 1954), pp. 302–3.
In emphasizing Hamlet's conflict between vengefulness and justice, G. R.
Elliott has also observed the passion motive in this scene and has com-
mented upon it generally as an inhibition to Hamlet's mission in exacting
true justice. See *Scourge and Minister, a Study of* Hamlet *As Tragedy
of Revengefulness and Justice* (Durham, N.C., 1951), pp. 64–70, and
passim. For Hamlet's use of "rant" as a spur to action in the player scene
as well as for his increasing failure so to use it successfully, see D. R. God-
frey, "The Player's Speech in *Hamlet*, a New Approach," *Neophilologus*,
July, 1950, pp. 162–69.

ideal of balanced emotion in dramatic artistry (the lines on the play), his emotional excess (the lines contrasting himself with the player), and finally the restoration of emotional poise in his decision on the mousetrap. This rerendering of the earlier design not only echoes and reinforces the theme slowly commenced in Act I, but gives its development a quickened forward movement.

The balanced emotion which ends II.ii quickly gives way in III.i, however, to the mood of Hamlet's best known soliloquy. "To be or not to be" becomes a stage in the already established alternation between affective extremes as it introduces reflection upon suicide. It is thus a return to the weariness and the sterility of two previous episodes—but for the uncertainty of dreams in death's sleep who would not find his quietus in the bare bodkin? Who would not end by sleep the shocks and heartache of the flesh?

Act III, scene ii is also considered a digressive scene, an excursion into the topical, but like the player episode of II.ii it is actually a meaningful element of the play. Mr. Knight has noted this and some related matters.[5] At this point Ham-

[5] He insists that the address to the players is not "an inessential" and observes that it "outlines in terms of stage artistry the conditions in which the play's major conflicts might be resolved. The Players are to control their passions. . . ." (p. 310). Mr. Knight states further that Hamlet's efforts at self-control "witness his inability to live his own artistic wisdom," (p. 311) and, agreeing with Roy Walker, calls attention to the proximity of Hamlet's lines on decorum in acting to Horatio's "passion's slave" speech (pp. 312–13). These observations, which also underlie part of my interpretation, occur in an essay which appeared in the enlarged edition of *The Wheel of Fire* (1949). I regret that I had only the 1930 edition at the time a draft of this chapter appeared in the *Modern Language Quarterly* for December, 1952. I noted Mr. Knight's contribution in a 1954 reprint of his 1949 edition and am happy to acknowledge it now. With his usual productive allusiveness Mr. Knight refers to the aspects of *Hamlet* which I have listed in this note, and employs them in a view of the tragedy which is quite different in scope and emphasis from mine. My

let again addresses the actors, and once more voices his creed
of affective balance: players, "in the very torrent, tempest,
and . . . whirlwind of passion" must "beget a temperance
that may give it smoothness," and the actor who tears passion to tatters is offensive to the soul. But there is also the significant warning against deficient feeling: "Be not too tame
neither." This strong episode is quickly followed by a choric
piece, Hamlet's key lines to Horatio which express plainly
both his ideal and the moral conception upon which the play
rests:

> and blest are those
> Whose blood and judgement are so well commingled
> That they are not a pipe for Fortune's finger

concern is to develop them and many others into a dominant and extensive
scheme which removes a traditional contradiction in the play; gives
new and unified meaning not only to the player scenes but to the Queen's
closet scene, the grave scene, and the Claudius-Laertes episodes; and furnishes what I regard as the major theme of the play. In Mr. Knight's essay
death is still the major theme and he remarks that all other elements are
subordinate to it (p. 299). Mr. Knight's reference to Roy Walker (see
above) is based upon a typescript of *The Time Is Out of Joint* (London,
1948), p. 71.
  That there is nothing entirely new under the sun is borne out, however, in some notes made eighty years ago by W. W. Lloyd who saw a
relation between the passion's slave speech, the lines to the players, and
several other passages which are central to this problem (*Critical Essays
on the Plays of Shakespeare*, London, 1875, pp. 426 ff.). He thus "anticipates" Mr. Knight, Mr. Walker, and myself on the starting point of
interrelated passages, but his point of view, which is neo-Coleridgean, is
no more an equivalent of our interpretations than they are equivalents
of one another. Lloyd's conception of Hamlet's flaw appears to be that
of a fatal moderation, not the tragic deficiency-in-excess of feeling which
I find expressed by both *Hamlet* and Hamlet. Completely apart from my
view is Charles D. Stewart's—that Hamlet *in fact* is incapable of emotion
(*Some Textual Difficulties in Shakespeare*, New Haven, 1914, pp. 204 ff.).
I hope I have made it plain that Hamlet only "senses" emotional dullness
which, in turn, induces passionate excess. I trust that this is also dis-
tinguishable from the rather standard Hamlet who suffers only a simple
excess of passion. See, for example, J. H. E. Brock's interpretation in
The Dramatic Purpose of Hamlet (Cambridge, 1935).

> To sound what stop she please. Give me that man
> That is not passion's slave, and I will wear him
> In my heart's core, ay, in my heart of heart,
> As I do thee.

As we have noted, there is a relationship between Shake-spearian tragedy and Elizabethan doctrines of passion which indicates that, whatever fault the present interpretation may have, it is not anachronistic. The "passion's slave" lines are central both to characterization and theme, and, as usual in Shakespeare, the timing is a major part of the emphasis: the speech to Horatio appears at a moment of quiet just after Hamlet's statement, in actors' terms, of its equivalent, and just before the climactic trapping of Claudius.

The play within the play soon follows. It should be observed that the Player King (III.ii.204 ff.) dwells upon shallow and short-lived passion ("What to ourselves in passion we propose . . .") which is followed by the Player Queen's pledges of solid and enduring love, and the real queen's sensing of the emotionally spurious note: "The lady doth protest too much, methinks." Then as the mousetrap is sprung Hamlet is thrown into great agitation, but at the scene's end he collects himself sufficiently to resolve upon restraint in dealing with his mother: "Let me be cruel, not unnatural."

But in its presentation of the passion theme, the play witnessed by the stage audience is not confined to a choric description of emotion dulled by mellowing time. It also expresses pointedly the accompanying irony of emotion blunted by its own violence. The Player-King's lines of exposition, which declare the "poor validity" of a purpose which soon weakens, are capped by this addition:

> The violence of either grief or joy
> Their own enactures with themselves destroy.

In this, the Player-King's lines express the contradiction of too little emotion in too much,[6] a contradiction already

[6] Stress in the play-within-the-play upon the principle of deficiency-in-excess of emotion or purpose is just as significant as emphasis upon the same theme in the Claudius-Laertes passages, which will be discussed later. In both cases Shakespeare is pointing up main action and main situation by parallel subaction and subsituation. It is therefore quite important to show that the paradox is actually stressed, not just mentioned, in the mousetrap play. Complete quotation of the choric passage under discussion reveals a most extensive *interaction* between strength of emotive dedication and its lapse or failure. And this is expanded by continuous reminder of fortune and fate through which not only passion or purpose, but everything else, contains and produces its own opposite or contradiction:

> But what we do determine oft we break.
> Purpose is but the slave to memory,
> Of violent birth, but poor validity;
> Which now, like fruit unripe, sticks on the tree;
> But fall, unshaken, when they mellow be.
> Most necessary 'tis that we forget
> To pay ourselves what to ourselves is debt:
> What to ourselves in passion we propose,
> The passion ending, doth the purpose lose.
> The violence of either grief or joy
> Their own enactures with themselves destroy:
> Where joy most revels, grief doth most lament;
> Grief joys, joy grieves, on slender accident.
> This world is not for aye, nor 'tis not strange
> That even our loves should with our fortunes change;
> For 'tis a question left us yet to prove,
> Whether love lead fortune, or else fortune love.
> The great man down, you mark his favourite flies;
> The poor advanc'd makes friends of enemies.
> And hitherto doth love on fortune tend;
> For who not needs shall never lack a friend,
> And who in want a hollow friend doth try,
> Directly seasons him his enemy.
> But, orderly to end where I begun,
> Our wills and fates do so contrary run
> That our devices still are overthrown;
> Our thoughts are ours, their ends none of our own:
> So think thou wilt no second husband wed;
> But die thy thoughts when thy first lord is dead.

depicted in the two previous player episodes and shortly to be found in the Queen's closet scene, the Claudius-Laertes encounter, and the grave scene. As we shall see, it is a paradox explicit throughout the play and of primary importance in the characterization of Hamlet.

Act III, scene ii thus presents in several forms the ideal of emotion suited to action or circumstance: Hamlet's lines to the players on decorum in acting, his lines to Horatio on slavery to passion, and his resolution of restraint toward Gertrude are all varied expressions of the same theme. In addition, the play-within-the-play emphasizes emotion weakened by time and by its own excess. And it is dramatically important that all this surrounds the structural climax of the play, the testing of Claudius; Hamlet's hour of decision and the multiple restatement of his affective ideal are nearly simultaneous. There could be no better preparation for the irony of later events.

The nature of this irony was dramatically defined in the player episode of II.ii; there Hamlet was shamed by the actor into emotive violence directed at his own deficient emotion, and doubly shamed by the violence itself, from which he recoiled in self-contempt. Thus when measured by his fervent ideal of balance (exemplified in Horatio) he is deficient; but he escapes deficiency only to become excessively and, to himself, ignominiously verbal. If we watch for final recurrence of this pattern, we shall find it in the grave scene. Prior to that point, however, it appears in III.iv, the "Queen's closet" episode, which avoids traditional confusion if the deficiency-in-excess irony is allowed to control its interpretation.

In the Queen's closet scene Hamlet rebukes his mother for

the false passion which accompanies carnality, and his flight
or, as it turns out, his descent, into rhetorical emotion again
becomes prominent. Whether intended as "antic" hysteria,
high indignation, prurience, or a combination of such qualities, Hamlet's intensity here is extreme. Yet in the midst of
it the ghost appears to "whet" his "almost blunted purpose."
Those who are skeptical of Shakespeare's coherence ask,
"What blunted purpose?" The necessary trap has been laid
and has done its work; Hamlet has been a shrewd avenger
in refusing to kill Claudius at prayer; and he is now at the
point of redeeming his mother. Nor has the killing of Polonius really deflected him. It has often been said that although these events may delay the revenge, they scarcely
imply a waning intent which the ghost needs to whet—that
there is nothing about them which could justify the Ghost,
Hamlet, or any one else in pointing to a dulled volition.
Hence Shakespeare is alleged again to have adapted the old
play in a confused manner. If the scene is considered in relation to what has gone before, however, Hamlet's blunted
purpose will be quite different from the pale delay assumed
as Shakespeare's intention by those who then confess failure
to find it in the action.[7] At the ghost's very appearance here
Hamlet has confessed himself a "tardy son . . . lapsed in
time and passion." If he is thus lapsed in passion, it cannot
be in the sense of retreating into sickly thought or lack of
conviction, for that would make nonsense of the cogency
which accompanied both his killing of Polonius and his

---

[7] Mr. Walker resolves the traditional contradiction in this scene by
finding that the Ghost has now changed from a spirit urging vengeance
to one urging mercy, i.e., now warning Hamlet of a blunted purpose
which lies in forgetfulness of mercy. (*The Time Is Out of Joint*, pp.
103-7.) The argument is interesting, but I cannot agree with it as an
interpretation of Hamlet's conflict of passion in this episode.

verbal attack on Gertrude, events which immediately pre-
ceded the ghost's arrival. Shakespeare deserves an attempt
at coherent interpretation, and coherence rests upon patterns established in previous action; the tardy son lapsed in
passion should be not the son whose passion has cooled,
but the one who has lapsed from duty while in a state of
passion,[8] the very act which made him turn in contempt
upon his own hysteria in the "rogue and peasant slave"
speech of II.ii. There he had fallen a-cursing like a very
drab; here he has given himself over to the berating of Gertrude. His "blunted purpose" at this point should again be
indignation or disgust cherished for its own sake, and in-
dulged verbally and wastefully.

"How all occasions do inform against me,/ And spur my
dull revenge!" In IV.iv Hamlet points to sleeping, feeding,

[8] Samuel Johnson apparently began the opposite, and perhaps standard,
interpretation (see Kittredge and the *Variorum*): "having suffered *time*
to *slip* and passion to *cool*." The Clarendon reading, however, provides
the meaning which I find supported by the context: "Or rather, the indulgence of mere passion has diverted him from the execution of
his purpose." I have been happy to find that this interpretation can be supported by Shakespeare's own usage:

> Two beggars told me
> I could not miss my way: will poor folks lie,
> That have afflictions on them, knowing 'tis
> A punishment or trial? Yes, no wonder,
> When rich ones scarce tell true. *To lapse in fulness*
> Is sorer than to lie for need, and falsehood
> Is worse in kings than beggars.
>   (*Cymbeline* III.vi.8–14; italics added)

"To lapse in fulness" obviously means to lapse while in a state of pros-
perity. By analogy, "lapsed in time and passion" would mean lapsed from
duty while in the double state of allowing time to expire and of indulging
passion. In his edition of *Hamlet* (Cambridge, 1936, p. lxiv) J. Dover Wilson accepts an equivalent of the Clarendon reading but does not cite
it or support his choice. G. R. Elliott does likewise except that, while
not resorting to other Shakespearian usage, he effectively uses the scene's
context as evidence (*Scourge and Minister*, p. 119).

and bestial oblivion as his lot, although examples gross as
earth exhort him. There are the lines about thinking too precisely on the event, but the complete passage presents a context of emotional dullness, not one of mental nicety, and
in dramatic interpretation the enveloping emphasis should
govern; the snatched-at phrase or clue is the least reliable
datum. The stress is upon the theme of emotional deficiency,
and Hamlet's concomitant fear of emotional excess is also
restated in the strong lines beginning, "Rightly to be great/
Is not to stir without great argument."

It is true that in addition to confessing a dulled sensibility
Hamlet declares here his inability to act (lines 43–46), and
it is apparent that this self-accusation receives little or no
support from the plot. For that matter, both deficient sensibility and deficient action may seem to be denied by a play
which presents Hamlet as feeling and acting to a remarkable
degree. But the issue, of course, is the kind of emotion and
the kind of action which the play presents, and there the
parallel is clear. With Hamlet a sense of emotional lack leads
to feverish emotion; a sense of inaction leads to feverish action. But deficient feeling far outweighs deficient action as
a motive and as a theme, and neither motive is even remotely
linked with neo-Coleridgean brooding or indecisiveness.

Act IV, scene v brings the return of Laertes in a scene
timed to follow the Fortinbras encounter of IV.iv, and thus
one foil device succeeds another. There are few better ways
of determining Shakespeare's intent than by noting such
oppositions. Readers of *Hamlet* are aware that Laertes' appearance on the scene introduces choler and dispatch; above
all, here is anger uninhibited by the quest for balance and
propriety of response. Act IV, scene vii provides a clear

statement of the Hamlet-Laertes contrast, as well as a restatement of the play's theme. As the subplot develops and
Claudius urges Laertes to revenge (lines 108 ff.), his lines
dwell at first upon the theme of sensibility blunted by time.

> *King.* Laertes, was your father dear to you?
>   Or are you like the painting of a sorrow,
>   A face without a heart?
> *Laertes.*   Why ask you this?
> *King.* Not that I think you did not love your father;
>   But that I know love is begun by time;
>   And that I see, in passages of proof,
>   Time qualifies the spark and fire of it.
>   There lives within the very flame of love
>   A kind of wick or snuff that will abate it,
>   And nothing is at a like goodness still;
>   For goodness, growing to a plurisy,
>   Dies in his own too much.

It should be noted that while dulled affections are treated
simply here at first, Claudius in his warning to Laertes
quickly comes to Hamlet's own paradox, deficiency in excess of feeling—goodness growing to a "plurisy" (fullness)
and dying "in his own too much." The passage continues,
moreover:

>   That we would do,
>   We should do when we would; for this "would" changes
>   And hath abatements and delays . . .
>   And then this "should" is like a spendthrift sigh,
>   That hurts by easing.

Again Claudius stresses the paradox of dulled emotion leading to "spendthrift" emotive catharsis, the "easing."
    The lines of Hamlet and the gravediggers which open
Act V have a quality of episodic digression, but any descrip-

tion of them is incomplete if it fails to account for context. The mood here is not dramatically static, for its de-
tachment lends a preparatory quality out of which Hamlet's
crisis at the grave (V.i.277) will come with great effect.
Although Hamlet's rash encounter with Laertes at the burial
of Ophelia is often explained as melodrama of Ur-*Hamlet*
descent, genetics are secondary to Shakespeare's use of the
incident for irony which caps the passion's slave theme and
seals Hamlet's failure. Here he confronts not only Laertes,
his foil, but Claudius and the dead Ophelia, and amidst her
"maimed rites" he faces everything he has hated and the
remnants of everything he has valued. His affective mettle,
which twice previously (II.ii and III.iv) has lapsed into the
shreds and patches of verbal anger, meets its last test, and
the outcome is exactly as before. Like the player's passion
of II.ii, Laertes' grief becomes a challenge to Hamlet's power
of response, and his retort to Laertes, like his reaction to the
player, is an "unpacking," an excess of emotive display.

> *Hamlet.* I lov'd Ophelia. Forty thousand brothers
>   Could not, with all their quantity of love,
>   Make up my sum. What wilt thou do for her?
> *King.* O, he is mad, Laertes.
> *Queen.* For love of God, forbear him.
> *Hamlet.* 'Swounds, show me what thou 'lt do.
>   Woo 't weep? woo 't fight? woo 't fast? woo 't tear thy-
>   self?
>   Woo 't drink up eisel? eat a crocodile?
>   I'll do 't. Dost thou come here to whine?
>   To outface me with leaping in her grave?
>   Be buried quick with her, and so will I;
>   And, if thou prate of mountains, let them throw
>   Millions of acres on us, till our ground,
>   Singeing his pate against the burning zone,

Make Ossa like a wart! Nay, an thou 'lt mouth,
I'll rant as well as thou.

Note especially Hamlet's words "to outface me," a pro-
vocative echoing of his shame in II.ii at being outfaced in
emotion by the player, who thus induced the "rogue and
peasant slave" soliloquy.[9]

Although this outburst parodies Laertes' extravagant grief
(lines 269–77), and although it expresses the humor which
often masks Hamlet's sense of tragedy, it is much more than
parody or macabre wit; [10] it would be a simplified interpretation which did not relate these lines to previous characterization. Even if Hamlet's spendthrift emotion in this scene
simply continues his feigned madness, the tragic result remains unchanged. If the excess is feigned, Hamlet is ironically the victim of his own craft which has forced him into

[9] Note also that in repenting his excess at the grave, Hamlet ascribes his
"tow'ring passion" to the "bravery" (showiness) of Laertes' grief (V.ii.
75–79).

[10] Mr. Walker's interpretation here is the opposite of mine. He finds in
Hamlet's lines an "outrageous mockery" of Laertes' grief and observes
that it is "the sort of rant Shakespeare would have given the First Player
if, as some suppose, he had wanted the Pyrrus speech to show as mere
melodrama" (*The Time Is Out of Joint*, pp. 137–38). I believe that
Shakespeare wished to show in Hamlet's response to the Player's tirade,
as well as in his response to Laertes' melodrama, an all too ready sympathy with emotional excess and violence. In both instances he is "outfaced," shamed, into duplicating the example before him. Nor can I
agree with Mr. Knight who finds Hamlet's ranting speech a "self-
critical" one, spoken with "controlled fury and cynical abandon" and
deriving from Hamlet's possession of genuine emotional intensity as well
as maturity. "Laertes is, in comparison, a child in emotional experience"
(*Principles of Shakespearian Production*, New York, 1937, pp. 170–71).
Mr. Elliott also finds Hamlet in control of himself here (*Scourge and
Minister*, pp. 171–74). Professor Schücking, however, suggests that Shakespeare actually inserted the churchyard scene as an afterthought, and that
one of his reasons for so doing was to reinforce Hamlet as a slave of passion in the tradition of Miss Campbell's interpretation ("The Churchyard
Scene in *Hamlet*, V.i, an Afterthought?" *Review of English Studies*, XI
1935, 129–38).

histrionics which he detests. If, on the other hand, the passion here is real, Hamlet in his own phrase of II.ii has indeed unpacked his heart with words. Finally, if his outcry against Laertes is a blend of the real and the feigned, the irony while more subtle is more acute: the antic disposition has induced a tragic habit, a form of emotive pretense which has at last grown to more than pretense. In any case, just as Macbeth was inwardly undone before Birnam Wood ever came to Dunsinane, so Hamlet is spent at this point. Playwriting modes of the time required that he undergo formal death in the ensuing scene, but within psychological limits there is really nothing left after this catharsis of passion. There remain but Osric, the poisoned sword, and silence. If the scene at the grave seems an indecorous catastrophe for Hamlet, we may recall simply and briefly the frequent conduct of Antony, Lear, and Timon, or that of Othello with Emilia's words, "fool," "gull," "dolt," ringing like a chorus. Shakespearian decorum in tragedy never softens the spectacle of folly.

I have no desire to make sweeping claims for unity in *Hamlet*. With those who feel that the play ends in accident, in a panoply of confusion and corpses which breaks the chain of motivation, I do not wholly disagree. But it is worth noting that Act V will gain in meaning if Hamlet's catharsis at the grave is seen as the completion of his inner tragedy, for after the grave scene it is perfectly fitting that the "external" Hamlet achieve revenge in a vacant world of accident.[11] To say it is fitting, however, is not to insist that the play carries its irony to such limits.

[11] In any event, I am among those who find nothing resembling dramatic emphasis on Hamlet's Christian reconciliation in Act V. If Hamlet is supposed to be like Lear, then Shakespeare has failed to dramatize it properly.

If the theme which unifies *Hamlet* is unnoted, the play will suffer both from looseness of structure and loss of forward movement. These disturbing elements will appear in II.ii, with the lengthy sampling of the players' wares which, if unconnected with the main action, will interrupt progress for some two hundred lines. Similarly, unless III.ii is related to the central theme, this critical scene will also contain a long topical digression, Hamlet's advice to the players upon acting. The lengthy interval from III.iv, through V.i, moreover, includes Hamlet's crisis with the Queen, Ophelia's madness and suicide, Laertes' arrival, and the grave scene. If this is viewed merely as Ur-*Hamlet* plot, without attention to imposed thematic development, it remains picaresque narrative which ends wanderingly in the burial of Ophelia.

Although the supposedly formless in *Hamlet* cannot be reshaped to the compactness of *Othello*, order and climax may take the place of confusion if we understand Shakespeare's efforts to express his theme, especially in the so-called digressive episodes. In Act I the theme is introduced and developed. In II.ii the world of drama calls up Hamlet's standards of affective restraint in the writing and staging of plays, and it then provides the setting for his first lapse into excess of feeling as an escape from deficiency. Then III.ii, the second player scene, allows Hamlet again to state his ideal of sensibility in actors' terms, and to voice it directly in the "passion's slave" lines to Horatio. Also, the play before Claudius dwells chorically upon waning passion, as well as upon the lapse of passion through its own extremity. In the long course from III.iv through V.i, the theme appears in the crucial "closet" scene and controls subordinate action through vivid reference, in the Claudius-Laertes passages, to the dulling of affections both by disuse and excess. Finally, the theme removes the scene at Ophelia's grave from the limbo of noisy anticlimax, for Hamlet's emotive waste in challenging Laertes' emotive powers is the ultimate expression of his conflict. It is the end of his flight from underresponse to overresponse which begins as early as II.ii, and approaches completion in III.iv, the Queen's closet scene. Thus may the tragedy be described in Elizabethan terms of passion and restraint; Hamlet's lines to Horatio become the key both to his standard of inner worth and his tragic failure to meet that standard. Just as significantly, if conflict of the passions is allowed to motivate Hamlet, dramatic action will augment self-revelation, and a unity between the two will be restored. The historical contradiction between character and plot will disappear.

vi. "Though you can fret me, you cannot play upon me"

IN Act III, scene ii, just after the mousetrap climax, there is a colloquy between Hamlet and the King's twin provocateurs, Rosencrantz and Guildenstern. The familiar subject of their dialogue is a recorder. Hamlet has forced Claudius to "unkennel" his guilt, an assortment of probers has attempted to penetrate the antic disposition, and at this point Hamlet probes two of the probers. These related events are scarcely explained by observing that the play contains prying and spying as natural elements of its plot, for the climax of unkenneling leads directly to thematic commentary. The recorder scene appears at the high point between the unmasking of Claudius and Hamlet's soliloquy of decision ("Now could I drink hot blood . . ."), and its function is to allow Hamlet to discourse elaborately, with the aid of a symbol, upon the sanctity of privacy and the right of complex personality to flourish without intrusion.

Re-enter one with a recorder.
Hamlet. O, the recorder! Let me see.—To withdraw with you:—why do you go about to recover the wind of me, as if you would drive me into a toil?

Guildenstern. O, my lord, if my duty be too bold, my love is too unmannerly.

Hamlet. I do not well understand that. Will you play upon this pipe?

Guildenstern. My lord, I cannot.

Hamlet. I pray you.

Guildenstern. Believe me, I cannot.

Hamlet. I do beseech you.

Guildenstern. I know no touch of it, my lord.

Hamlet. 'Tis as easy as lying. Govern these ventages with your finger and thumb, give it breath with your mouth, and it will discourse most excellent music. Look you, these are the stops.

Guildenstern. But these cannot I command to any utterance of harmony. I have not the skill.

Hamlet. Why, look you now, how unworthy a thing you make of me! You would play upon me, you would seem to know my stops, you would pluck out the heart of my mystery, you would sound me from my lowest note to the top of my compass; and there is much music, excellent voice, in this little organ, yet cannot you make it speak. 'Sblood, do you think that I am easier to be play'd on than a pipe? Call me what instrument you will, though you can fret me, you cannot play upon me.

Here Hamlet's flippant but pointed lines express a theme of the play just as his "passion's slave" speech expresses another.[1] From the recorder passage it is plain that inner sensibility is to be valued for its own sake; the presumption, moreover, of one consciousness upon another is not a right but a privilege based upon respect for "compass" and "mystery."

[1] The speech to Horatio, incidentally, occurs immediately before the play's climax; the recorder passage, as we have noted, comes immediately after. The two passages are related, moreover, in that the recorder lines are anticipated by the "pipe for Fortune's finger" metaphor in the address to Horatio.

The recorder lines sum up this note in the tragedy, and our concern will be to trace what may be called the recorder theme from its initial statement in Act I to its formulation in Act III as part of the climax.

It is now understood that the Ghost in *Hamlet* was something new in revenge-play usage.[2] Unlike the spirits in *The Spanish Tragedy* and the Ur-*Hamlet* [3] who met actors and audience man-to-man, Shakespeare's apparition is one of sensitivity and reserve. It is "offended" at Horatio's pardonable but untimely "What art thou . . . ?/ By heaven I charge thee, speak!" (I.i.46 ff.). It "stalks away," and on its reappearance Horatio drops his initially jarring note for a formalized, incantatory one:

> But soft, behold! Lo, where it comes again!
> I'll cross it, though it blast me. Stay, illusion!
> If thou hast any sound, or use of voice,
> Speak to me;
> If there be any good thing to be done
> That may to thee do ease and grace to me,
> Speak to me;
> If thou art privy to thy country's fate,
> Which, happily, foreknowing may avoid,
> O speak!
> Or if thou hast uphoarded in thy life
> Extorted treasure in the womb of earth,
> For which, they say, you spirits oft walk in death,
> Speak of it; stay, and speak!

But at cockcrow, symbol of public day, the spirit who was about to address the watchers (see I.ii.215–220) shrinks and vanishes.

[2] See J. Dover Wilson, *What Happens in Hamlet* (Cambridge, 1951), Chap. III.
[3] *Ibid.*

Plainly the elder Hamlet is represented by a ghost who resists the time-tried forms of "drawing people out." A nineteenth-century critic might have ascribed Hamlet's own resentment at being played like a recorder to an inherited family trait. The similarity between father and son may be brought more to the point, however, by noting that the Ghost dramatically reflects Hamlet's ideal of character and is therefore a fitting symbol, like Horatio in the "passion's slave" lines, of personal qualities which Hamlet values beyond price. In addition, the Ghost is a telling instrument of exposition and so may be expected to introduce notes which appear later in the play.[4]

The reticence of the spirit, its quality of withholding self-revelation from those who must earn and await what they seek, reappears in the vivid confrontation scenes (I.iv and v). There, in response to Hamlet's great invocation, the Ghost simply beckons and Hamlet follows it slowly off stage, so that scene v begins with son and father-apparition alone for the moment of confidence. The disclosure is made and the Ghost's previously secretive role is now assumed by Hamlet; as the watchers press him for news, he deflects their inquiry with the "wild and whirling words":

> *Horatio.*   What news, my lord?
>
> .   .   .   .
>
> *Hamlet.* There's ne'er a villain dwelling in all Denmark—
>   But he's an arrant knave.
> *Horatio.* There needs no ghost, my lord, come from the
>   grave
>   To tell us this.

[4] See the end of Chapter VII for the role of the Ghost in establishing the "antic" theme.

Hamlet.   Why, right, you are i' the right.
  And so, without more circumstance at all,
  I hold it fit that we shake hands and part;
  You, as your business and desire shall point you,
  For every man has business and desire,
  Such as it is; and for mine own poor part,
  Look you, I'll go pray.

Following this come Hamlet's announcement of the antic disposition and the long oath of secrecy which is augmented by remote echoes of "swear" from beneath the stage.

We have moved from Act I, scene i to scenes iv and v in order to sense fully the aloof and self-contained nature of the Ghost; we have also recalled that Shakespeare's stress upon these qualities probably departed from revenge play tradition. In scene ii Hamlet makes his first appearance. At this point he neither possesses a secret, nor has he assumed a curiosity-inciting madness, so that his only motive is to fend off the probing of his grief. And actually there is no real probing in the solicitous though heavy-handed inquiry. Yet Hamlet reacts with gnomic parrying; from the very first his response to other characters resembles his later irritation at recorder players. The hearty address of Claudius, "But now, my cousin Hamlet, and my son," the direct approach of Gertrude with her platitude that death is common, and the question, "Why seems it so particular with thee?" are met with secretive contempt and *double entente* in the "too much i' th' sun" and kin-kind lines, in the snappish "Ay, madam, it is common," and in "Seems, madam! Nay, it is; I know not 'seems.'" Hamlet has "that within which passeth show," and as he listens to gusty aphorism for some thirty lines, his resentment accumulates so that its utterance in the "too too

solid flesh" soliloquy comes with climax and catharsis. The
passage ends: "but break my heart, for I must hold my
tongue."

None of this, I trust, will be taken to mean that Hamlet
would accept incestuous parents if they would only stop in-
quiring into his welfare. The incest and haste of the marriage,
we assume, are naturally insupportable. But so is the inquiry,
the recorder playing, and in I.ii it is this which "touches off"
the deeper resentment. A good dramatist understands that
characterization depends upon such precipitative factors.
They, not the moral attitudes of a character, are the primary
indicators of temperament; the trigger mechanism, not the
explosive charge, reveals the firearm's quality.

It would be easy to find the note of clumsy-fingers-on-the-
recorder in I.iii, with Laertes and Polonius at work upon the
sensibilities of Ophelia, but I prefer to deal with correspond-
ences which seem striking and effective. Otherwise, analogy
flattens with proliferation so that everything, and conse-
quently nothing, takes on "meaning." If we are to deal with
collateral action as a basis for the current theme, it is better
to choose an aspect of the subplot which is pointed and rendered to the purpose. We find it at the beginning of Act II in
the scene between Polonius and Reynaldo.

The first half of this scene seems vividly direct in its thematic character. In advancing the plot it merely calls attention to Laertes' arrival in Paris so that his later entry may take
the form of a dramatic return, and it is clear that an episode
so limited in narrative function could have succeeded with
almost any subject for incidental dialogue. Yet the subject
turns out to be the familiar one of recorder playing, the invasion of private sensibility by ponderous devices. Polonius,

who in I.iii could advise his son to be zealously reticent with those who would merge his life with theirs, here incites Reynaldo, the *agent provocateur*, to enter the most intimate aspects of Laertes' life. This is to be done, moreover, by weakening the reserve, the loyal caution, of "Danskers" Reynaldo may find in Paris who, after being played upon, will unwittingly "close" with him "in the consequence" and reveal Laertes gaming, or falling out at tennis, or entering "such a house of sale,/ *Videlicit*, a brothel, or so forth." In terms of the recorder theme, Polonius dwells with fascination upon the fingering of difficult instruments and simply succeeds, as we know, in framing gaudy platitude on the interviewing of reluctant witnesses. Reynaldo by "encompassment and drift of question" is to find out who knows Laertes; then he is to indicate "as 'twere, some distant knowledge of him." Next he is to lay "slight sullies on my son,/ As 'twere a thing a little soil'd i' the' working." Thus will come the closing in the consequence and the unwitting admission. Polonius finally pronounces his imbecile peroration, a generalized prescription for the death of privacy:

And thus do we of wisdom and of reach,
With windlasses and with assays of bias,
By indirections find directions out.

It is plausible enough, moreover, to believe that Reynaldo, obviously the craftsman played upon by an elderly novice, is having his own sensibilities dragged to the surface. He listens, is actually shocked when Polonius suggests "drabbing" as a conversational gambit for drawing out Laertes' friends ("My lord, that would dishonour him."), and when finally forced to respond to the inane pressure as Polonius asks, "You have me, have you not?" replies, "My lord, I *have.*" From the context, a director of the play could in clear conscience supply the italics.

The remainder of II.i, a reporting of Hamlet's new role by Ophelia, is similar in one respect to the Polonius-Reynaldo encounter: again, the plot function is a very simple one— the course of Hamlet's antic behavior is to be revealed. Just as Polonius and Reynaldo could have talked about anything interesting so long as they implied the arrival of Laertes in Paris, so here Ophelia could have described Hamlet's mad conduct in any of a dozen ways so long as she established its appearance. But it happens that Ophelia, like Polonius and Reynaldo, is given lines which strongly support the recorder theme; her description of the antic Hamlet centers upon an anguished, wordless attempt by one character to assess the depths of another:

> He took me by the wrist and held me hard;
> Then goes he to the length of all his arm,
> And, with his other hand thus o'er his brow,
> He falls to such perusal of my face
> As he would draw it. Long stay'd he so.
> At last, a little shaking of mine arm.
> And thrice his head thus waving up and down,
> He rais'd a sigh so piteous and profound
> That it did seem to shatter all his bulk
> And end his being. That done, he lets me go;
> And, with his head over his shoulder turn'd,
> He seem'd to find his way without his eyes,
> For out o' doors he went without their help,
> And to the last bended their light on me.

One can say that this is simply melodramatic adoration, tragic leave-taking, or artful madness. True, except for "simply." The manner of the adoration, the farewell, or the madness, is one of exploring, invading, evoking. Is the audience "aware" that Hamlet's searching of Ophelia recalls Horatio's importuning of a silent ghost, or Polonius' fantastic scheme for "closing" with Laertes? Hardly, and it makes little difference; aware or not, the audience is becoming accustomed to a theme, and a clear formulation of it will follow. Such a preparation for later development is the method, whether conscious or intuitive, of the artist.

Thus with the conclusion of II.i, the theme of invasive soul-searching, soon to be capped by the recorder lines, has been presented perhaps more consistently than any similar element of the play. From this point it expands. That the expansion is a function of probing, detection, and exposure in the plot in no way makes the theme redundant; plot and theme, like plot and character, will correspond with one another, but it does not follow that they will equal each other or that the agreement between them will be unimportant. Plot is based upon unity of events, while theme stems from unity in the coloration of events. Theme is a matter of ideas, attitudes, values—of commentary, express or implied. The plot of *Othello*, for example, stresses the making and breaking of reputations, but the reputation theme in *Othello* is not its mere equivalent.

The developments of Act II which follow Ophelia's account of Hamlet continue the familiar note. As Hamlet's new and strange cast of mind appears, it in turn is subject to search and divination. Polonius, whose comic quest and surmise here is well known, "looses" his daughter as a provocation, and his own psychic defenses, such as they are, go down before Hamlet's antic cross-examination in the "fishmonger" passage. The King and Queen, who are not quite sure of Polonius, augment the forces at work by employing Rosencrantz and Guildenstern to "glean" the inner state of Hamlet, who in his first encounter with them defends himself by flaunting the complexity they seek to probe. The man who finds public Denmark a prison could have his privacy bounded in a nutshell, and count himself the king of infinite space, were it not that he has bad dreams. And as he accuses Rosencrantz and Guildenstern of being "sent for," he baffles them further with his lines on the intricate piece of work called Man.

As the mousetrap scene is approached the recorder theme evolves profusely. In quick succession appear Hamlet's probing of himself (the "rogue and peasant slave" soliloquy),[5] the decision to use the play which will tent Claudius to the quick, and the report by Guildenstern on the antic disposition, which he explains as Hamlet's device for evading questions concerning his "true state." Then comes the catechizing of Ophelia in the "nunnery" scene and, ultimately, the climax itself, the penetration into "occulted guilt" by means of the play. Finally, and directly associated with this, occurs the recorder episode in which the cumulative meaning of prior action and commentary is given ex-

[5] I have no notion whether Shakespeare "intended" the congruity between soliloquies in which Hamlet tents himself to the quick and the repeated situations in which one character is tented to the quick by another. The reductivist is always sure that there was no such intention; the enthusiast is usually convinced that there was; the freewheeling critic scorns the issue of intent. I do not scorn it. I believe, however, that a practiced dramatist will arrive at such consistency intuitively, and I cannot see intuitional performance as unintentional, except in the most uselessly literal sense. The intuitive unity is in the play and it is up to the responsible literary historian to describe it.

On the presence in *Hamlet* of constant analysis, a probing into various ideas, see F. C. Kolbe, *Shakespeare's Way* (London, 1930).

pression. Hamlet calls for the instrument at the moment of the mousetrap success and dwells upon it as a symbol.

Through the history of Shakespeare criticism Hamlet, the character, has gradually become isolated as a symbol of self-examination, of inner consciousness quizzically brought to view and dissected. As we know, an unfortunate result of this tradition has been a diminished interest in the play as it supports the character. In returning to this larger interest, however, we need not sacrifice a concern for the introspective Hamlet if we recognize an inclusive theme of private consciousness probed crudely or skillfully, comically or tragically, justly or unjustly—a process which involves not only Hamlet but the entire cast, and one which affects every major incident except the last scene.

As for light on Hamlet's character, I trust that the implications of the recorder theme are clear enough. One specific observation, however, is in order. For all his revulsion at being psychically played upon, Hamlet remorselessly plays upon himself and is fated to explore and lacerate the inner state of others: Polonius on the comic side; Rosencrantz and Guildenstern on the serio-comic level; Claudius, Ophelia, and Gertrude on the plane of seriousness. Such a fate he accepts readily, and more often than not with a perverse joy. If we are pressed for his motive we may say that he does not shrink from the invasion of privacy but from the invasion of complex privacy by clumsy and conventional devices. Such is the strict meaning of the recorder passage; Hamlet's disgust there is leveled only at a musicianship of the simple-minded.

vii. *"To put an antic disposition on"*

NINETEENTH- and early twentieth-century critics of Shakespeare deal variously with Hamlet's madness. Some tell us that he assumes the antic disposition to relieve an overwrought mind, some consider his behavior clinically, and others, anticipating present trends, declare that the madness is purely feigned because that is the way Hamlet describes it. We are told also, of course, that we must preserve Hamlet's sanity if we wish to preserve him as a tragic hero. And inevitably among the older critics we encounter theories of actual madness or instability coexisting with feigned madness. Students of Shakespeare are aware that the issue is a highly documented one. A reading of the *Variorum* section, "Is Hamlet's Insanity Real or Feigned," followed by a scanning of references in Raven's *A* Hamlet *Bibliography and Reference Guide*, will remind anyone of the range and intensity, the occasional near-sublimity, and the frequent nonsense of the controversy. It is impossible to contribute something new to this question without repeating some historical answers, but older theories in revised form, and with additional evidence, can be useful and valuable if they are presented in a fresh relationship to the text of the play.

When we turn from a history of the problem to modern standards of interpretation, we find the academic view expressed in hand books or anthologies of Shakespeare designed for college use. This position rejects nineteenth-century subjectivism and abandons the old habit of considering Shakespeare's characters apart from the plays in which they appear. It also limits *Hamlet* to a conventional simplicity and directness. Hazelton Spencer, for example: "The theater is a temple of conventions, and among those which Shakespeare built into *Hamlet* were the avenger's assumption of madness while biding his time. . . . Hamlet is not mad for a single moment; he is playing mad." [1] And the editors of a widely used edition:

There is no question whatsoever about Hamlet's sanity; his madness is only feigned. His decision to put an antic disposition on when and as he shall see fit, is taken suddenly (I.v.168 ff.), and he never gives any reason for it. This is not the case in Belleforest, where the feigned madness is clearly motivated. There Hamlet, a mere youth, pretends madness as a protection against an uncle who would slay him without hesitation if he could be sure of his sanity. How the madness was motivated in the lost play we do not know. But in Shakespeare, where the deed of Claudius is not known, and where Claudius is eager to be on good terms with Hamlet, this device is not necessary. The fact would seem to be that Shakespeare accepted the feigned madness as an integral factor in his inherited material, either without realizing that with his re-creation of the hero it needed a different motivation, or without caring to invent one. Very likely Shakespeare believed that audiences in the playhouse would be content to assume that Hamlet had reasons of his own. Certainly he knew that the feigned madness would afford moments of comic relief, for he uses it most skillfully to that end. Though Hamlet utters "wild and whirling words"

[1] *The Art and Life of William Shakespeare* (New York, 1940), p. 314.

on a few occasions when it is clear that his speech is not a display of the antic disposition (e.g., I.v.117 ff.; III.ii 282 ff.; V.i.297 ff.), his conduct at such times is no more than the recoil from emotional strain, such as any normal person might exhibit. To particularize briefly, if the nonsensical jingle which Hamlet spouts after the success of the "mouse trap" betrays a neurotic state, we should certainly expect Hamlet to be highly excited when instructing the player in the delivery of the lines he has composed for him and in talking with Horatio before the play begins; but then he is conspicuously calm. For his unseemly conduct at Ophelia's grave he manfully repents; the showy grief of Laertes revolted him and made him forget himself.[2]

In this reading of *Hamlet* the antic theme not only lacks support from character motivation but its very presence in the play is a contradiction. The contradiction is explained largely by genetics through which we learn that the feigned madness, logically employed for the hero's self-protection in the source, illogically survives in the play as the opposite of self-protection. In attempting an affirmative contribution, I hope to imply that *Hamlet* is its own defense against this standard view of the matter.

In the first part of this chapter I shall try to show that real and feigned "ecstasy" [3] coexist in the Queen's closet scene, and that their merging at this stage of the play is prefigured in early exposition (I.iv and v). I shall also suggest that the

[2] Neilson and Hill, eds., *The Complete Plays and Poems of William Shakespeare* (Boston, 1942), pp. 1045–46. By permission of Houghton Mifflin Co.

[3] Although Shakespeare is unsparing in his use of the word "madness," I shall generally use "ecstasy" which is the Queen's term (see III.iv), because it avoids modern clinical connotation in which eccentricity, neurosis, and insanity are distinguished. The question of madness in the modern sense of psychosis is to be avoided. "Ecstasy" will do very well.

exposition combines the recorder theme with the antic theme in such a way that protection of privacy becomes one of Hamlet's motives for the antic disposition. Next, I shall point to the fusion of real ecstasy, feigned ecstasy, and the recorder theme as it is found in remaining parts of the play. Finally, I shall show briefly that Hamlet's assumption of the antic disposition is a turning point at which the play itself, in tone, event, and characterization, suddenly assumes the new, the antic, quality of its hero, and is thenceforth controlled by the antic theme.

I

In III.iv Hamlet kills Polonius, berates Gertrude, and again confronts the Ghost. From the quality and structural position of this scene we may assume that its presentation of the madness theme will be definitive. If so, clear irony is the result; there can be no doubt that Hamlet attempts to convince his mother that he is sane, but his efforts seem to be self-nullified at every turn. As the Ghost enters, the Queen plainly points to Hamlet's countenance and behavior:

> Alas, how is't with you,
> That you do bend your eye on vacancy
> And with th' incorporal air do hold discourse?
> Forth at your eyes your spirits wildly peep,
> And, as the sleeping soldiers in th' alarm,
> Your bedded hairs, like life in excrements,
> Start up and stand on end. O gentle son,
> Upon the heat and flame of thy distemper
> Sprinkle cool patience. Whereon do you look?

As Hamlet seeks to explain what Gertrude thinks is hallucination, she remarks upon his ecstasy, and his reply is a vehement attempt to correct her impression which, of course, would be an obstacle to the moral mission he has undertaken:

> Ecstasy!
> My pulse, as yours, doth temperately keep time.
> And makes as healthful music. It is not madness
> That I have utt'red. Bring me to the test
> And I the matter will re-word, which madness
> Would gambol from. Mother, for love of grace,
> Lay not that flattering unction to your soul,
> That not your trespass, but my madness speaks.

If the irony of this scene were limited to an awesome ghost inducing a state which Hamlet had previously feigned, it would be both obvious and unremarkable. Many see the ecstasy in III.iv as entirely caused by the Ghost, and would describe Hamlet's behavior as "no more than the recoil from emotional strain, such as any normal person might exhibit." [4] They scarcely have considered the closet scene as a whole; if we turn to the beginning of it we find the irony of a feigned state turned real presented long before the Ghost's entry. When the Queen and Polonius open the scene in preparation for Hamlet's entrance, we hear him from "within," and as he approaches to redeem his mother, a duty which should require him to cast off the antic disposition, we might expect some lines of sober thought or at least an entry which would show a "private" Hamlet dramatically minus his public eccentricity. Instead we hear his weird cry from off stage, "Mother, mother, mother!" As he appears, there follow some lines of stichomythia which in their formality contrast madly with the wild and whirling words before his entry. Hamlet's demeanor and stilted,

---

[4] See the standard opinion, quoted on page 88.

clipped speech so terrify the Queen that she exclaims, "What wilt thou do? Thou wilt not murder me?" and her cry for help brings the cry of Polonius from behind the arras with its immediate and well-known consequences. Now, after a laconic farewell to the "wretched, rash, intruding fool," Hamlet blandly calls upon his mother to sit down for his speech on the two pictures, which he delivers as though the accidental stabbing of a lord chamberlain were the normal prologue for a sermon on marital purity. As the rhetorical violence mounts into lines on "the rank sweat of an enseamed bed,/ Stew'd in corruption," and the "honeying and making love/ Over the nasty sty," the Ghost finally enters and we have Hamlet's vacant eye and hair-on-end look which induces the dialogue, already noted, on his ecstasy. But in the midst of this upheaval, and hence with characteristically mad aplomb, he can offer as proof of sanity his pulse, which "as yours, doth temperately keep time,/ And makes as healthful music." Thereupon he concludes his moralizing and weaves into it a last claim to feigned rather than actual madness:

> *Queen.* What shall I do?
> *Hamlet.* Not this, by no means, that I bid you do:
>   Let the bloat king tempt you again to bed,
>   Pinch wanton on your cheek, call you his mouse,
>   And let him, for a pair of reechy kisses,
>   Or paddling in your neck with his damn'd fingers,
>   Make you to ravel all this matter out,
>   That I essentially am not in madness,
>   But mad in craft. 'Twere good you let him know;
>   For who, that's but a queen, fair, sober, wise,
>   Would from a paddock, from a bat, a gib,
>   Such dear concernings hide? Who would do so?

No, in despite of sense and secrecy,
Unpeg the basket on the house's top
Let the birds fly, and like the famous ape,
To try conclusions, in the basket creep,
And break your own neck down.

Had Shakespeare desired a clear-cut Hamlet who could
assume or discard his eccentric role as the need arose, this
is the point at which the antic would have been notably
absent. The passage itself is a disclaimer of madness (see the
eighth line) and it comes after the sequence of lines (149–
179) in which Hamlet has settled into self-contained, sympathetic discourse on continence and has expressed sober re-
pentance for the killing of Polonius. The antic disposition
has been dropped completely in this thirty-line segment of
the scene.[5] But at line 180, upon the Queen's "What shall I
do?" at which we could expect a continuing of the discursive, almost gentle tone, the antic role returns with startling
effect in the very passage which denies it. Hamlet lurches
into speech which is indistinguishable from the cryptic
and flippant prurience, the ironical expression of idea in
terms of opposite idea, and the adducing of gnomic, fabulous,
and fragmented illustration which previously have marked
his antic discourse with Polonius, Rosencrantz and Guildenstern, Ophelia, the King, and the Queen herself. Under no
circumstances do what I now tell you to do. Let the King
pinch and paddle; tell him that I am but mad in craft—be
sure to do this (" 'Twere good you let him know"), for who,

[5] This should answer the interpretation which finds Hamlet "saving"
his mother in the closet scene, but still "hedging," i.e., protecting himself
by appearing mad lest she prove treacherous. His desire to disclose himself to her as sane and responsible is the prime note of the scene, a fact
which also answers those who find Hamlet feigning madness to make his
moralizing more poignant and spectacular.

that's merely a queen would think of hiding such precious
matters from a toad, a bat, a tomcat? "Who would do so?"
No, behave like the ape on the housetop who let the birds
fly out of the basket: climb into the basket, try to fly out,
and break your motherly neck. Had Polonius lived a few
moments longer to hear Hamlet's disclaimer of madness, he
would have sensed a mad ring to it, with which he had become quite familiar. But even Polonius would have found it
hard to say that the disorder had method in't. Hamlet's insistence to Gertrude that his madness is but "in craft"
strangely lapses into the mad exterior, the manner of the
craft; the mask is lifted to show a duplicate mask underneath.
Had Polonius been spared he might well have said again,

> to define true madness,
> What is't but to be nothing else but mad?
> But let that go.

Nor does the ecstasy end here. As Hamlet and his mother
exit, there is his line, "I'll lug the guts into the neighbour
room," which is introduced with puns on the corpse that
shall set Hamlet "packing" (see Kittredge) and on the prat-
ing Polonius now being "most grave," —all to the accompaniment of "Mother, good night . . . Good night,
mother." At the opening of the next scene we have Gertrude
declaring to Claudius that Hamlet is "mad as the seas and
wind, when both contend/ Which is the mightier."

Reductive interpreters would explain this declaration by
Gertrude as simple obedience to Hamlet's command that
she conceal the feigned nature of his madness. They also
would describe the lugging of corpses to a chant of puns and
good-nights as a device for clearing the stage. And they
would add that the antic disposition was used inconsistently

as inherited material, so that the Hamlet whose ecstasy denies his disclaimer of it comes as no surprise. Polonius, it happens, is also a reductive critic; in paraphrase, he would have agreed that to hear Gertrude conceal Hamlet's feigning, what is't but to hear her conceal it. To be a user of stage conventions for the removal of corpses, what is't but to be a user of stage conventions? And to be derivative from old plots, what is't but to be nothing else but derivative? It is Polonius' "nothing else," of course, which limits him; those who feel that an oversimplified historical method is a disservice to history may take heart from Shakespeare's own satire.

In short, if we sense not the reduced but the manifold context of Gertrude's "mad as the seas and wind" speech, we hear her partly as dutifully deceiving the King and partly as wondering whether she is not, after all, telling the truth. If we sense a dual purpose for Hamlet's exit "tugging in Polonius," we begin to see that devices for clearing the stage could simultaneously convey meaning. (Was Lear's exit pursued by attendants and remarked upon by the Gentleman as a "sight most pitiful," just a device for clearing the stage?) Finally, although we may know that Shakespeare set the old feigned madness in a new and apparently contradictory situation, we may suspect that he made something of the contradiction. None of this leads to esoteric interpretation; we are merely entertaining complexity in a Shakespeare character who is nothing if not complex, and who has just played his strange role in a very strange scene. Shakespeare's audience, moreover, probably savored strangeness more than literary genetics and would have been delighted to witness a new twist to the old antic disposition theme.

We have begun with the Queen's closet scene because it
presents the antic disposition in full development. Since
it shows true ecstasy breaking through Hamlet's claim of
false madness, the presence in opening exposition (I.iv and
v) of a directly parallel scheme will suggest a design. At the
very introduction of feigned madness into the play, real
ecstasy becomes the medium of its disclosure. Even before
the Ghost enters there is the prophetic note on madness
struck in Horatio's lines:

> What if it tempt you toward the flood, my lord,
> Or to the dreadful summit of the cliff
> That beetles o'er his base into the sea,
> And there assume some other, horrible form,
> Which might deprive your sovereignty of reason
> And draw you into madness? Think of it.

It is well known that Hamlet's "wild and whirling words"
after meeting the Ghost precede his decision to "put an
antic disposition on," but the full extent of his aberration at
this prefeigning point has not been appreciated. In addition
to his familiar sense-in-nonsense ("There's ne'er a villain
dwelling in all Denmark—/ But he's an arrant knave," or
"I hold it fit that we shake hands and part;/ . . . Look you,
I'll go pray."), the quality Horatio finds wild and whirling,
there is another odd note, a suspicious and reiterative defensiveness, which runs through Hamlet's lines. In the interval between his return from the Ghost and his decision to
feign madness he becomes divided between a desire to remain alien and yet to share his experience with others. It is
interesting that this conflict is suggested by earlier exposition (I.ii) in which Hamlet, after secretive word-play with
Claudius and the Queen, ends his first soliloquy with the

line, "But break my heart, for I must hold my tongue" and
shortly expresses relief at the encounter with Horatio, Marcellus, and Bernardo, friends with whom shared experience
is possible. Now, in I.v, when the Ghost has revealed a
murder and Hamlet's wild words ensue, the same conflict
appears, this time on a plane of psychic disturbance. Here
is a gathering of the friends who previously furnished the
release of sharing; here is the sharing again in a rite of
secrecy and the confided antic disposition. But a new quality
is present, a distempered suspicion addressed to those in
whom Hamlet had formerly placed his trust. The singularity
does not lie in his insisting upon an oath of secrecy; it appears
in the manner of the insistence, at once rapt, laconic, repetitive, and automatic,[6] a manner, moreover, which has succeeded the unstrung state of "Hillo, ho, ho boy! Come bird
come."

Hamlet's morbid suspicion within his ceremony of trust
and confidence begins with lines addressed to Horatio and
Marcellus: "No, you'll reveal it" (the Ghost's disclosure)
—"But you'll be secret?"—"Never make known what you
have seen tonight"—"Nay, but swear't"—"Upon my
sword." At the civil reply, "We have sworn, my lord, already," there is the impatient "Indeed, upon my sword indeed," followed by "Come on; you hear this fellow in the
cellarage./ Consent to swear," and as the Ghost's echo inter-
rupts, there is an immediate return to the demand: "And lay

    [6] G. R. Elliott notes the "fantastic scrupulosity" of Hamlet's in-
sistence in this scene upon the oath, and also calls attention to the
"proud, inhuman, and irreligious solitude" which characterizes Hamlet's alienation and secretiveness at this point and elsewhere (*Scourge
and Minister*, pp. 35, 38, and *passim*). Under the circumstances, I cannot
find the solitude inhuman, nor can I see in the play an emphasis upon its
irreligious quality.

your hands again upon my sword./ Never to speak of this
that you have heard,/ Swear by my sword." Then the con-
spiratorial warning in an anxious form which will appear
again in the Queen's closet scene (never do what I suggest
you are likely to do):

> But come;
> Here, as before, never, so help you mercy,
> How strange or odd soe'er I bear myself,—
> As I perchance hereafter shall think meet
> To put an antic disposition on—
> That you, at such time seeing me, never shall,
> With arms encumb'red thus, or this headshake,
> Or by pronouncing of some doubtful phrase,
> As "Well, we know," or "We could, an if we would,"
> Or "If we list to speak," or "There be, an if they might,"
> Or such ambiguous giving out, to note
> That you know aught of me,—this not to do,
> So grace and mercy at your most need help you,
> Swear.

Even in the midst of an exit with the bond of sharing established, the quirk appears again. First come the calm and
gentle lines:

> Rest, rest, perturbed spirit! So, gentlemen,
> With all my love I do commend me to you;
> And what so poor a man as Hamlet is
> May do, t' express his love and friendling to you,
> God willing, shall not lack. Let us go in together.

But between this well-poised passage and the three final lines
on a time which is out of joint can recur suddenly the
nervous reminder, the anticlimax in one of the most climactic
oaths of secrecy ever taken: "And still your fingers on your
lips, I pray." Actually, the confiding Hamlet has revealed

next to nothing; despite one of the ten demands of silence
which runs, "Never to speak of this that you have heard,"
the watchers have heard very little indeed. They have seen
something, but the initial question, "What news, my lord?"
has never been answered. For sound and politic reasons, of
course; the point here is not one of Hamlet's shrewdness
but of his aberrant manner. Upon his encounter with the
Ghost, and as a prelude and accompaniment to announcing
the feigned madness, he transcends the normal reticence of
I.ii with a new state of anxious, repetitive riddling, an ecstasy
of self-concealment. With this, the antic disposition becomes linked with the privacy or recorder motive.

II

Our concern is chiefly with the unity of *Hamlet* and we
may now begin to relate part to part and part to whole.
Hamlet's ecstasy is fully established prior to his putting on
of the antic disposition; it thus appears from the exposition
that his decision to feign the antic arises within an antic
state,[7] and that the feigned and the real are as firmly combined as they will be at later points such as III.iv. In addition,
the antic disposition merges with the recorder theme. Real
ecstasy, simulated ecstasy, and ecstatically cherished privacy
are thus aspects of one another, and are made so at an early
stage of the play. If with doubtful wisdom we ask whether
Hamlet is really mad, the answer in Hamlet's terms is that
he is mad north-northwest of pretended madness; if we in-
quire why he exhibits the antic disposition the answer lies

[7] The point is sometimes made that Hamlet "probably" had worked
out his plan of feigned madness prior to announcing it in I.v. It is a
point no audience would catch and one which confuses the acts of a
real person with those of a fictional character.

south-southeast of the recorder motive: the antic is a protection against those who would play him like a pipe. If we
are asked "to distinguish more clearly," the reply may have
to be that we know a hawk from a handsaw. The ecstasy
in I.v. is not feigned; the "madness" present when Hamlet
baits Polonius is superbly feigned; and Hamlet's first defense of his privacy against the King and Queen (in I.ii)
contains a mere suggestion of the antic. These situations,
however, are among the few which can be so described;
through most of *Hamlet* the false antic, the real antic, and
the recorder motive are appropriately blended to produce a
manifold character in a many-sided play.

The appearance in *Hamlet* of a protective feigned madness which simply stirs up suspicion and danger is not, therefore, the anomaly so often noted, for Shakespeare apparently
altered his source extensively in order to supply coherence
between the old theme and the new situation. In Shakespeare
the antic disposition is no longer a device to prevent others
from *acting* against Hamlet; instead it serves to baffle in-
quirers who are always fascinated by idiosyncrasy and try
endlessly to uncover "that within which passeth show."
Feigned ecstasy, moreover, is a defense against the consequences of real ecstasy, against recorder players who will
inevitably explore an unbalance which Hamlet, after his
meeting with the Ghost, knows he cannot conceal. Exploit
the antic disposition, then, to the limit; augment the real
with the false. The stratagem works until in the closet scene
with the Queen it begins to work too well.

Have we reverted here to the Romantic Hamlet? Have we
revived the distraught soul who plays at being mad because
his madness must have release? Only, I think, in a thoroughly

modified and unsentimental sense: Hamlet never indulges a "malady." His real disturbance is at hand to break through; his feigned disorder can be called upon to protect his privacy. The true and the false, however, have a habit of mingling, as they must in an active imagination.

It is interesting that belief in Hamlet's wholly feigned ecstasy is largely expressed by characters who are both hostile and deluded. On the other hand, the reality of his unbalance is usually asserted by characters who at least attempt a sympathetic understanding. If we examine this distinction we shall find that it involves a further combining of the antic and recorder themes.

"I'll board him presently. . . . How does my good Lord Hamlet?"—with these words Polonius in II.ii begins to play the recorder but is stopped on his opening note by the antic disposition. The fishmonger, the daughter who may not walk in the sun, and the eyes of old men purging plum-tree gum do their work of confusion. Hamlet's encounter with Polonius is followed by his meeting with Rosencrantz and Guildenstern, who in turn are parried by the lines on Denmark as a prison, the infinite space within a nutshell, and the piece of work which is man. Thus, directly out of two gauche attempts to fret Hamlet's pipe comes a multiple and dubious discovery that his madness is pretended; Polonius, as every one knows, remarks on the "method in 't," while Rosencrantz and Guildenstern, report that it is "crafty." Claudius, moreover, anticipates their conclusion by asking whether they have found why Hamlet "*puts on*" this confusion." If the meaning of a play could be determined by canvassing dramatis personae for their opinions, the purely feigned madness of Hamlet might be established at this point. On the other hand, if playwriting were a form of double-talk in which clear statement means its opposite, the real madness of Hamlet could prevail. Neither of these conclusions, of course, would take account of the complexity within simplicity which good dramatic art contains.

A dramatic motive can be ambiguous, but in a good play this will be revealed by nonambiguous means. Shakespeare suggests that Hamlet's pretense is doubtful by "establishing" it through probers who are spotlighted to the audience as clumsy violators of privacy, simple schemers whose lack of insight is a distinguishing trait. These characters, moreover, flourish without hesitation or complication. Polonius "penetrates" the antic disposition within two short scenes after Hamlet announces it, while Rosencrantz, Guildenstern, and the King assert their skepticism at the beginning of Act III. Thus before the play is half over the wholly feigned ecstasy is clear to those who never question themselves because they are sure that recorders are very easy to play. They are devotees of the "first convolution."

What, now, of the characters who respect Hamlet's intricacy, who try to understand rather than to "glean" his mystery? In various ways they all declare he is mad or in danger of becoming so. Horatio's fear that Hamlet may be driven insane by the Ghost, and his coinage of the phrase "wild and whirling" are suggestive. Beyond this, however, he has nothing to say on the subject, a silence which fits his character; easy explanations hardly suit him. Through Ophelia is shown the most disturbing side of the antic disposition, and her outcry after the "nunnery" scene that "a noble mind is here o'erthrown" is one which engrossed

spectators can be relied upon to take seriously and to remember. Some may say to themselves at this point, "He's
mad, really mad!" but most will probably think, "What is
happening? Is it possible that real madness . . . ?"[8] Very
few, if any, will remind themselves that source-study provides a skeptical answer. Finally, to turn from Ophelia to
the Queen, the difficulty she, and we, have with the question
has already been described in discussing the closet scene.
There, to paraphrase Touchstone, the truest ecstasy is the
most feigning.

Within Act III the mixture of feigned madness, real ecstasy, and the recorder theme continues as we approach their
complete union in the recorder episode. Just after the trap
is closed upon Claudius comes one more anticipation of the
closet scene phenomenon in which feigned ecstasy is con-
tinued beyond the point of any useful, protective purpose.
After the play of Gonzago has unkenneled the usurper's
thoughts, the stage is emptied of all but Hamlet and Horatio,
between whom no feigning ever exists. Yet the antic disposition, as we know, continues in full force:

> *Hamlet.* Why, let the strucken deer go weep,
>   The hart ungalled play;
>   For some must watch, while some must sleep,—
>   So runs the world away.
>   Would not this, sir, and a forest of feathers—if the rest
>   of my fortunes turn Turk with me—with two Provincial

---

[8] Insanity is supposed to have been comic on the Elizabethan stage, but
this tradition must be qualified by an equally prominent convention: the
comic could also be pitiful and terrible. No matter what view, historical
or otherwise, is taken of the "nunnery" scene the outrage upon innocence
is so startling and Ophelia's response so genuine that momentary audience
impressions will outweigh all others. There is far more ecstasy here,
moreover, than is necessary for the mere antic deception of Claudius and
Polonius.

roses on my raz'd shoes, get me a fellowship in a cry of
players, sir?

Horatio. Half a share.

Hamlet. A whole one, I.

> For thou dost know, O Damon dear,
>   This realm dismantled was
> Of Jove himself; and now reigns here
>   A very, very—pajock.

Horatio. You might have rhym'd.

To say that these lines are antic is not to imply that they lack
cogency, for Hamlet's feverish observations are always pertinent and meaningful. As usual, the antic quality lies not in
the thought but in its wild and whirling utterance.

The passage just quoted may suggest an ecstasy, a condition of shock, the manic phase of a manic-depressive psychosis, a humor gone "adust," or several other states, de-
pending upon the critic's lexicon. Names do not matter. So
far as dramatic art is concerned, however, it is the perfect
projection of a mood surrounding the play's climax, the
unmasking of Claudius. The timing, moreover, is as apt as
the passage itself, which we may therefore take seriously
without being guilty of "clue snatching." At this turn of
plot, with its call for "lights, lights, lights!" as though to
reveal all that is hidden in Denmark, there is a dramatic
change from feigning to actuality. Through most of the
mousetrap scene the antic state of Hamlet has been public,
and hence tactical, but as the stage is cleared Hamlet, Horatio, and the audience are left "privately" to savor the guilt of
Claudius. Here a dramatist who had wished to make
feigned madness certain could have done so once and for
all by presenting Hamlet in a mood of coldly rational anger.
The contrast would have been eloquent. But the opposite of

this occurs; Shakespeare extends the antic disposition into a situation where it can scarcely be pretended, and presents real ecstasy in a form indistinguishable from the feigned.

Rosencrantz and Guildenstern reenter in preparation for the recorder scene, and the feigning pattern is again in order. But as before the pattern undergoes no change. In the gyrating manner of the strucken deer—forest of feathers —Damon dear—pajock lines, Hamlet with one look at the interlopers, shouts for music, for the recorders, and continues the rime and jingle celebration of his discovery.

> For if the king like not the comedy,
> Why then, belike, he likes it not perdy.

He repeats the cry for music. There now follow some fifty lines of solemn antic, and, "reenter one with a recorder." Shakespeare might have led Hamlet into his thematic speech immediately, but he does it thus:

> O! the recorder! Let me see—To *withdraw* with you.

The wonderful mock-conspiratorial touch—the retirement into whimsical privacy (it excludes only Horatio) for a heart-to-heart talk about a wooden pipe. And as the audience is fascinated by this cloak-and-whistle tête à tête, the recorder passage, Hamlet's final assertion of the privacy theme, comes in terms of the antic disposition and as a fitting expression of triumph over Claudius and the spies. "Call me what instrument you will, though you can fret me, you cannot play upon me"; at this Polonius enters and Shakespeare concludes the mad episode with Hamlet's passage on the cloud, the camel, the weasel, and the whale, lines which express the antic in a mock fretting of the Lord Chamberlain's pipe.

Thus, within III.ii, a scene in which feigned and real ecstasy have been merged, the recorder note has been struck
as an essential part of the climax. Hamlet has assembled the
probers—Claudius, Rosencrantz, Guildenstern, and Polonius. The tables of probing have been turned; the King has
been "tented," Rosencrantz and Guildenstern have been
lectured on their obtuse methods, and Polonius has been
cross-examined in a miracle of nonsense. Hamlet's first impulse following the mousetrap has been to repay recorder
fretters in kind, with the antic disposition in full play. It is
only after this that he turns to the crisis at hand.

> Now could I drink hot blood,
> And do such bitter business as the day
> Would quake to look on.

Oddly but characteristically, these lines immediately follow
the lampooning of Polonius.

Between the Queen's closet scene and the grave scene
comes Ophelia's madness, which sets forth another recorder
facet of the antic theme. The episode could have been presented without officious inquiry, but the recorder note is
kept prominent; first there is a report by the Gentleman that
Ophelia "speaks much of her father" and that her "unshaped"
speech, accompanied by "winks and nods and gestures," has
caused all hearers to "aim at it" and "botch the words up
fit to their own thoughts." Horatio then agrees that the
surmises may be dangerous. So the probing begins, but it
is far from clear, perhaps deliberately, what the probing
is for; discovery that Ophelia is unstrung over the death of
her father is the solemn Polonian verdict of Claudius who
begins by indirections to find directions out, and deduces
the already obvious from an airy nothing.

King. How do you, pretty lady?
Ophelia. Well, God 'ild you! They say the owl was a baker's
    daughter. Lord, we know what we are, but know not what
    we may be. God be at your table!
King. Conceit upon her father.

In lines following this, however, Ophelia suggests with
mad balladry on betrayed love something which is missed
by Claudius but caught by most interpreters from Coleridge
to Kittredge: her madness reflects her rejection by Hamlet.
And in the next phase of the scene the same suggestion arises.
Here the distraught Laertes comes close to sensing the allusion:

Ophelia. You must sing, "Down a-down, and you call him
    a-down-a." O, how the wheel becomes it! It is the false
    steward, that stole his master's daughter.
Laertes. This nothing's more than matter.

The "investigation," however, ends without result. Claudius
has sought a conclusion which required no seeking, has
found it, and has missed completely any finer shade of meaning. Ophelia's mad scene thus perpetuates the hunt for motives of madness by those who are mad with tautology and
common sense; although a collateral episode, it preserves
the close connection in *Hamlet* between the antic theme
and the recorder theme.

Act V brings the gravediggers and the brawl with Laertes.
Although the gravediggers are not cut in the pattern of Tom
of Bedlam, their function is similar, and it may be recalled
that the *pièce de résistance* in this feast of sallies between two
naturals and an antic Hamlet is the skull of Yorick—"a
whoreson mad fellow's it was" too. In this mood Shakespeare
prepares for the maimed rites of Ophelia and the "scene" at

the grave. Should one, at this stage of the play, insist upon a
Hamlet who is only feigning, there are three problems with
which to contend. First, on the literal plane of realism it
would seem clear that any protective or calculated reason
for pretending madness has long since vanished. The King
has already sought Hamlet's death and Hamlet knows he
will do it again. The probers, moreover, have run their
course. Secondly, the grave scene depicts the abandoned
grief of a character who could no more sustain calculated
feigning than he could avoid physical struggle with a chief
mourner who "outfaces" him in an exhibition of sorrow.
Finally, there is the problem of audience response; as Hamlet
reveals himself at the grave, there is the cry of Claudius,
"O, he is mad, Laertes," which a practiced dramatist knows
will influence most spectators. It is conceivable, that one
or two will recall the King's fear of exposure from Hamlet,
and see Claudius as feigning belief in the unfeigned nature
of Hamlet's feigned madness. But that, to put it mildly, is
hardly the way plays are meant to be understood. It is in
this scene that Hamlet's genuine unbalance breaks through
with finality, and here, it will be recalled from Chapter V,
is also the terminal point of his drift from deficient emotion
into tragic excess of feeling.

In discussing the substance, manner, and dramatic development of Hamlet's antic disposition, I hope that I have never
pointed to Shakespeare's tragedy as a clinical study of madness or even as a play about a clearly mad hero. Where the
pretended ecstasy becomes "real," the reader or spectator
is privileged, of course, to draw his own conclusions, but
if he attends to the play it seems to me that his response will

be one of questioning surmise. The enigma is paramount, and
if it is disregarded the tragedy becomes a document, a case
history. In presenting the issue of doubt, however, Shakespeare is the dramatist from first to last. There is no confusion, no enigma, in the staging of enigma, for the mixture
of real and feigned ecstasy is presented in a form which is
at once orderly, cumulative, and effective. That there is
no "solution" is also made clear; this is the very point, the
actual function, of the recorder theme. No amount of pipe-
fretting will penetrate the mystery but the enduring fact of
mystery is before us with all the clarity which the stage
demands.

Nevertheless, it should be recalled that whatever the extent of Hamlet's ecstasy, the distracted hero, like Lear, re-
covers in preparation for death. Osric who is mad in the
socially accepted sense appears, arranges for the duel, and
brings upon himself the baiting which is Hamlet's last assertion of the antic disposition. This is accompanied by full
self-possession which recalls the aberrant but poised hero
of Act I, scene ii. He is ready: "If it be now, 'tis not to
come. . . . Since no man has aught of what he leaves, what
is't to leave betimes? Let be."

III

In conclusion, we may consider the antic theme as it
controls the play. Upon its introduction in I.v with the
wild and whirling words of Hamlet, it suddenly transforms
not only the hero but the medium through which he appears.
Prior to I.v all characters, including Hamlet himself, are
presented with the conventional seriousness of tragedy; after
that point it is a different story in which the roles of the

Ghost and Polonius are of special interest. Until the concluding lines of Act I all appearances of the Ghost have
been solemn ones. With Hamlet's putting on of the antic,
however, the figure who had earlier appeared "with solemn
march" and with "slow and stately" movement, the spirit
who had led Hamlet to the moment of revelation with silent
"wafting" and had made his disclosure in the diction of
grand tragedy, suddenly becomes the "old mole," a kind
of poltergeist burrowing in the earth and popping *hic et
ubique* into the oath ceremony with echoes of the word
"swear." With the antic in Hamlet simultaneously appears
the antic in the Ghost.

On another plane, that of the subplot, the same transformation occurs at the same stage of the action. In II.i
(again, immediately after the antic disposition is introduced)
Polonius, who in Act I had been allowed the dignity of a
lord chamberlain and gentle father, suddenly becomes the
ubiquitous booby in high place. Absurdly and pruriently
lecturing Reynaldo, he finally bogs down with "What was
I about to say? By the mass I was about to say something."
It is true that in stage production, efforts have been made to
render Polonius comic in I.iii so that his turn to the ridiculous
with Reynaldo in II.i will not be a departure from established
characterization. Of this, two qualifications must be made.
First, the lines given Polonius in I.iii, especially those of
farewell advice to Laertes, are too good to be rendered as
nonsense. When Shakespeare portrays rhetorical asininity
the lines themselves are incompatible with anything else:
witness Armado, Dogberry, Bottom and others, including
Polonius from Act II onward. Second, there is no need in
Hamlet to "prepare" the Polonius of I.iii for his new role

in II.i, because preparation is provided through departure into the antic by Hamlet and the Ghost. At this point in fact, most of Denmark's court is transformed from the decorous assemblage of I.ii into a collection of "agents" prowling on egregious missions which always end in the baiting by Hamlet of imbeciles and unfortunates. This is the mood which governs most of the tragedy; even the death scene is arranged for by the unwitting and witless Osric. It is against an antic background that the antic Hamlet is presented and, as in *Lear*, tragedy is signaled by the sudden appearance of Bedlam, a transformation which affects simultaneously both the hero and his dramatic environment.

viii. *"Reputation, reputation,*

reputation!"

AS a principle which controls character and action in *Othello* the reputation theme has two aspects which are morally opposed but psychologically related. The first of these is an objective, "normal" regard for esteem and honor; the second is an inverted, egoistic defensiveness of good name which arises when esteem or honor is threatened. In the beginning of this chapter the double reputation theme will be described as it determines the play through Act III, scene iii, the "temptation" episode. Later, the egoistic side of reputation will be discussed as it affects Othello's tragedy of ritual dedication which will recall another tragedy, that of Brutus. The distinction I assume between the opposite aspects of reputation, as well as a validity of the distinction in Elizabethan tradition, is made clear in G. R. Elliott's definitive study of the sin of pride as a controlling force in *Othello*. Mr. Elliott differentiates between Othello's "right self-esteem" and "wrong pride," and equates with the most malignant form of pride what I call the egoistic pole of reputation.[1]

[1] *Flaming Minister, a Study of* Othello *As Tragedy of Love and Hate* (Durham, N.C., 1953). See the Introduction, and specifically pp. xxxiii, 117, 129, and *passim.*

I

Othello's first appearance in the play is a refutation of slander. In I.ii his conduct in facing Brabantio's party ("Keep up your bright swords . . .") nullifies the "thick lips," the "lascivious Moor," of earlier dialogue and lays a foundation for the council scene in which Othello gains a respect close to veneration. Thus, a deserved reputation, casually sensed by its possessor and pointedly accepted by others, answers the scurrility of Iago and Brabantio. Othello's easy bearing of his good name, his lack of egoistic concern for it, introduces the normal or objective aspect of the reputation theme.

It is Cassio, however, who brings the theme explicitly into the play: "Reputation, reputation, reputation! O, I have lost my reputation! I have lost the immortal part of myself, and what remains is bestial. My reputation, Iago, my reputation!" These lines are given added point by Othello's rebuking of Montano at the time of Cassio's disgrace:

> What's the matter
> That you unlace your reputation thus,
> And spend your rich opinion for the name
> Of a night-brawler?

Both this passage and Cassio's fervent words occur at high points of the scene (II.iii) in which Iago discredits Cassio, so that dramatic force is lent to thematic statement. Reputation becomes the "immortal part" of man, without which he is "bestial," a state well understood to color Shakespeare's portrayal of tragic depths; we may recall Hamlet's phrase, "a beast, nor more," and the chorus of animal imagery which accompanies the tragic descent in *Lear*.

Purely on the face of it, Cassio's lament might imply the egoistic pole of reputation. Only its distraught quality, however, would suggest this, for the passage and its context are free from the cankered defensiveness of Iago and Brabantio. Cassio blames no one but himself and indulges in no recrimination; in all simplicity and modesty he joins Desdemona in her plan to restore his position. Only once in the action leading to III.iii does Cassio show a morbid concern for reputation, and this occurs when he is drunk. In a memorable display of the concern for status shared by tipplers past and present, he says that he wants no more of Iago's singing, and announces (portentous *non sequitur*) that "there be souls must be saved, and there be souls must not be saved." He for one, "no offence to the general, nor any man of quality," hopes to be saved.

> *Iago.* And so do I too, Lieutenant.
> *Cassio.* Ay, but, by your leave, not before me; the lieutenant
> is to be saved before the ancient.

Reputation, reputation! This is Cassio's single and brief "Iago-phase" in which good repute is measured by standards of precedence and "face." When he becomes sober he sets out equably to redeem his lost good name.

Thus, in the first two acts Shakespeare presents his theme in a dramatic triumph by Othello over slander, and in an equally dramatic loss of honor by Cassio which is amplified by strong lyrical expression. In these episodes reputation is asserted within its sound and normal limits. But there is also its inverted aspect; if we return to the beginning of *Othello* we may follow a parallel stressing of good name in the form of self-regard and prideful delusion.

This plane of honor is suggested by Iago's familiar opening

speech on the preferment of Cassio, the "counter-caster" who "had th' election":

> He, in good time, must his lieutenant be,
> And I—God bless the mark!—his Moorship's ancient.

Brabantio shows a similar quality. A glance at his lines in the street encounter of I.ii will show that his sorrow and anger come not so much from the loss of a daughter as from public humiliation, from loss of reputation. In accusing Othello he protests the "general mock" which Desdemona has incurred by shunning "the wealthy curled darlings" of Venice in her choice of a Moor and an outlander. But it is Iago who fully expresses reputation in its malignant form. Shakespeare has him end two scenes, I.iii and II.i, in parallel soliloquies which clearly express his cast of mind. Brooding upon imagined injury, he cherishes fictions which enhance his degradation and justify retaliation; thence he moves from skeptical pleasure in these fictions to a consuming belief in them.

Iago's passage at the end of I.iii discloses among other things that his hatred of Othello turns upon reputation: "And it is thought abroad that 'twixt my sheets/ He has done my office." Iago does not know "if't be true," but led on by self-interest, he dismisses the question of truth: "But I, for mere suspicion in that kind/ Will do as if for surety." Here motive is expressed in soliloquy, and it is probably because of the deliberative air thus given Iago that he is often considered a cynic whose deceit is wholly calculated.[2] In a superficial sense this may be true but it is far from the

[2] This view is, of course, the opposite of S. A. Tannenbaum's who believed that Iago discloses the sober truth about Othello and Emilia, and that such truth is confirmed elsewhere in the play. "The Wronged Iago," *Shakespeare Association Bulletin*, XII (1937), 57–61.

whole truth when the soliloquy is read as part of a sequence (I.iii–II.i): obsessed with reputation—with what is "thought abroad"—Iago will actually suggest the later Othello as he passes naïvely from surmise to the delusion of certainty. Bystander at the affectionate greeting of Desdemona by Cassio, he is at first cynically conscious of his tactics: "With as little web as this will I ensnare as great a fly as Cassio. Ay, smile upon her, do; I will gyve thee in thine own courtship." And as he broaches the idea of adultery to Roderigo (II.i. 220 ff.), even that dupe can say what Iago has always known: "With him! why, 'tis not possible. . . . I cannot believe that in her; she's full of the most bless'd condition." But in his role of deceiver something happens to Iago that places him, for the moment, even below Roderigo's gullish level. In his prurient, knowingly false description of Desdemona he is a prototype of all virtuosos who play upon others at the price of playing upon themselves: "Mark me with what violence she first lov'd the Moor. . . . When the blood is made dull with the act of sport, there should be again to inflame it and to give satiety a fresh appetite, loveliness in favour, sympathy in years. . . . Now for want of these requir'd conveniences, her delicate tenderness will find itself abus'd, begin to heave the gorge, disrelish and abhor the Moor." And of Cassio: "a knave very voluble; no further conscionable than in putting on the mere form of civil and humane seeming, for the better encompassing of his salt and most hidden loose affection." These lines to Roderigo have a double function. On the surface, their excess of image and epigram expresses Iago's conscious attempt to deceive Roderigo; just beneath the surface the same effusion is part of Iago's unconscious deception of himself.[3] Somewhere in the course of his zeal a deliberate fiction (the adultery) has become to him, and him only, the truth. As the dialogue with Roderigo ends, Iago reveals his transformation in the soliloquy which concludes II.i.

> That Cassio loves her, I do well believe't;
> That she loves him, 'tis apt and of great credit.

And in the same passage another fiction becomes real. In the parallel soliloquy which concludes I.iii Iago had said of Othello's rumored affair with Emilia, "I know not if 't be true," and had casually assumed its truth for pragmatic reasons.[4] Now (at the end of II.i) the rumor is stripped of all indifference:

> For that I do suspect the lusty Moor
> Hath leapt into my seat; the thought whereof
> Doth, like a poisonous mineral, gnaw my inwards.

Iago's tactical aplomb, lost for the moment, will naturally return, for irony of self-deception requires self-assurance.

[3] Mr. Elliott effectively observes a form of self-deception in Iago's attempt to deceive Roderigo in this scene, but declares that Iago is unable to believe what he says about Desdemona at the end of II.i, the point at which I feel his self-deception becomes dramatically complete (see the ensuing discussion). Mr. Elliott reads Iago's words, " 'tis apt and of great credit" (II.i.296), as expressing a "plausible" idea which Iago knows is false (*Flaming Minister*, pp. 71–74). I doubt that this rather subtle meaning is made clear by Shakespeare.

Richard Flatter believes that Iago in this sequence has the "mentality of a crazy actor"—the ability simultaneously to believe and not believe the role he plays (*The Moor of Venice*, London, 1950, pp. 39–47). I partly agree, except for the emphasis Mr. Flatter seems to place upon the clever, light-hearted balminess of Iago's impression here on the audience. The distinction is important.

[4] The soliloquy which expresses this motive occupies a terminal position in I.iii which makes it directly analogous to the soliloquy concluding II.i. The structural parallelism and repetition of effect give an added force to the second passage, which thus recalls the first.

For background on Iago's motives in these soliloquies, see L. L. Schück-

But his fabricating of Desdemona's sin and his careless surmise about Emilia's, all because of a slight to his reputation,[5] have here grown to actual, fervent belief in the misdeeds of both women. Those who wish may link this behavior with paranoia, although Shakespeare would have called it a delusion of Pride. In any event, the process is confined to no single era or place, nor is it esoteric—Iago's motive is "motiveless malignity" only in the sense of his having no objective reasons for his disturbing belief. The disturbance begins with his mounting rhetoric directed at Roderigo; it becomes dramatically clear in the soliloquy which follows. And it is well understood that the summation of motive in soliloquy should not be taken lightly.

Since Act III, scene iii of *Othello* is the traditional point of disagreement between psychological interpreters and those who stress the "calumniator believed" convention, an old question may take on new meaning if we examine the scene for its unusual expression of the reputation theme. Concern for good name is made prominent here at two stages. The first is a passage (lines 130 ff.) in which Iago crosses the danger line and, half in duplicity, half in real

---

ing, *Character Problems in Shakespeare's Plays* (New York, 1922), pp. 207–11, and E. E. Stoll, *Shakespeare and Other Masters* (Cambridge, Mass., 1940), pp. 234–38. Mr. Schücking's view is similar to Mr. Elliott's (see note above). Mr. Stoll grants that Iago's soliloquy suspicions become convictions but is characteristically inclined to discount any psychological significance or consistency in this. My stress is upon the soliloquies as the beginning and end of a psychological pattern which includes Iago's self-deception in his eager attempt to deceive Roderigo. As a corrective to the older view of Iago's soliloquies see Marvin Rosenberg's recent and perceptive article, "In Defense of Iago," *Shakespeare Quarterly*, VI (1955), 145 ff., especially 152 ff.

[5] John W. Draper points out that Iago was compelled to act on rumor by the current code of honor. "Honest Iago," *PMLA*, XLVI (1931), 724–37. This is not at all incompatible with Iago's sudden and naïve belief in the rumor.

fear, retreats from Othello's questioning. Then, as Othello presses his tempter, Iago dramatically counters with simulated virtue; he cannot utter his "thoughts" because reputation is privileged, and—"Good name in man and woman,/ dear my lord,/ Is the immediate jewel of their souls."

The second appearance in III.iii of the reputation theme is equally forceful. It occurs just after Iago's avowal that "not poppy, nor mandragora,/ Nor all the drowsy syrups of the world" shall restore Othello's "sweet sleep." Othello resigns himself:

> O, now, for ever
> Farewell the tranquil mind! farewell content!
> Farewell the plumed troops and the big wars
> That make ambition virtue!

The passage then expands into further symbols of lost career and renown until it ends with "Othello's occupation's gone!" a dramatic echo of Cassio's "Reputation . . . I have lost my reputation!"

It should be clear that neither Iago's invoking of good name nor Othello's withdrawal from public honor is purposive here unless the reputation theme is assumed to be significant. In a run-of-the-mill scene involving temptation to jealousy, Iago's false reluctance would probably take the form of simple concern over drawing Othello into error, and Othello's agony would more aptly appear as a farewell to love instead of to martial glory. Shakespeare, however, turns both situations into lyrical developments of reputation, and so continues a theme which has been present from the beginning. Nor should it be forgotten that the episode is set in motion by Desdemona's move to redeem Cassio's good name. A scene presenting the reputation theme as it affects two characters (Desdemona and Othello) thus arises from efforts to restore the reputation of a third character.

Just prior to the lines on good name and the stolen purse Iago warns Othello:

> I do beseech you—
> Though I perchance am vicious in my guess,
> As, I confess, it is my nature's plague
> To spy into abuses, and oft my jealousy
> Shapes faults that are not—that your wisdom yet . . .
> Would take no notice. . . .

Ironically, because here he is consciously the deceiver, Iago has again told the truth about himself, the truth which appeared earlier as he passed from doubt to a belief which could gnaw his "inwards," and as he suddenly accepted his own false account of Desdemona's infidelity. Iago's lines on the "plague" of his nature thus depict the morbid or paranoidal aspect of reputation. But immediately, scandalously, comes the idealized good name speech. And just as unexpectedly, it in turn is followed by another assertion of morbid honor:

> That cuckold lives in bliss
> Who, certain of his fate, loves not his wronger;
> But, O, what damned minutes tells he o'er
> Who dotes, yet doubts, suspects, yet soundly loves!

At which Othello: "O misery!" But the focus changes again with Othello's recovery as he scorns "exsufflicate and blown surmises,/ Matching thy inference," rejects jealousy as a response to Desdemona's social graces, and concludes: "No, Iago;/ I'll see before I doubt; when I doubt, prove." Recovery, however, merely precedes relapse. "I'll see before I doubt" expresses simple normality, but "when I doubt, prove" is full of ambiguity; it can mean either that doubt

will wait for proof or that doubt will impulsively create
proof. The latter is the undermeaning which Iago immediately confirms as he supplies "proof" by reminding Othello
that Venetian wives "let Heaven see the pranks/ They dare
not show their husbands," and that Desdemona, after all,
deceived her father. At this, doubt and proof become one
with the response, "I am bound to thee forever," later to be
mocked by Iago in the last line of the scene: "I am your
own, forever."

The second phase of III.iii continues the shuttling, both
within and between characters, of opposite aspects of the
good-name theme. Othello reenters at Iago's line, "Look,
where he comes." The egoistic side of honor then gains full
expression as Othello declares he has been set "on the rack,"
that " 'tis better to be much abus'd/ Than but to know't a
little."

> What sense had I of her stol'n hours of lust?
> I saw 't not, thought it not, it harm'd not me.
> I slept the next night well. . . .

Ignorance of slander, a state of being "much abus'd," is now
valued above public good name. Concern for the outward
world has lapsed:

> I had been happy, if the general camp,
> Pioners and all, had tasted her sweet body,
> So I had nothing known.

Reputation is rejected, but its egoistic counterpart remains.
The play of contraries is resumed, however, for directly out
of Othello's abandonment of outward honor comes a statement of its priceless quality: "Farewell the plumed troops
and the big wars/ That make ambition virtue! . . . and all
quality/ Pride, pomp, and circumstance of glorious war!/

. . . Farewell! Othello's occupation's gone!" In the logic which controls III.iii, and extends throughout the play, strong affirmation and strong negation imply each other. This, of course, is a logic of the emotions but it represents an actuality of thinking and feeling which is a traditional basis for tragedy.

As with the original "good name" passage and its sequel, egoism now completes the pattern. Just as Othello had previously declared for objective proof ("when I doubt, prove"), so here after the line on occupation his demand runs, ". . . be sure thou prove my love a whore/ Be sure of it. Give me the ocular proof/ . . . Make me to see 't; or, at the least, so prove it/ That the probation bear no hinge nor loop/ To hang a doubt on . . ." And as before, objective proof becomes subjective delusion. The proof must be "ocular proof," and it appears as ocular fantasy: "Would you, the supervisor, grossly gape on—/ Behold her topp'd?" The "probation" must "bear no hinge or loop/ To hang a doubt on," and it consists of Iago's obscene account of Cassio's dream. Finally, again the ocular proof: "Have you not sometimes seen a handkerchief/ . . . such a handkerchief—/ I am sure it was your wife's—did I today/ See Cassio wipe his beard with." Upon introduction of the handkerchief the deception of Othello is complete: "If it be that, —"; and following these ominous words come the lines invoking "black vengeance" and "hollow hell."

A few remarks upon an old topic may now be offered. What is the motivation of Othello in the temptation scene? It is very doubtful that we have a case history in which the Othello of Acts I and II shows progressive traits which forecast his descent in III.iii. But whether we have such a de-

sign or not, a psychological theme has been dominant from
the start of the play. This theme, reputation, has appeared
in its two aspects of normal regard for good name and egoistic, defensive concern for "face." Iago has embodied the
latter side of the theme, and his morbid view of reputation is
the one which finally possesses Othello in III.iii.[6] Othello
has shown no previous morbidity, but the audience has become "used" to the trait as Iago, obsessed with reputation,
has dwelt first ironically and then with malignant conviction
upon the rumor about Othello and Emilia. The obsession
growing, he has spawned a rumor of his own, the Cassio-
Desdemona slander, and has suddenly disclosed in soliloquy
that he believes it also. In the temptation scene a clearly
similar process is enacted with Othello as the victim. As the
contrary aspects of reputation meet in a kind of dramatic
dialectic, the Captain, tensed by his regard for good name,
assumes the previous pattern of the Ancient: first the surmise, then the play of fancy in which slander is confirmed
by yet more vivid slander, and finally the delusion. But what
of the objection that motives of one character cannot be
extended to another? One must answer that only a literal
theory of motivation confines the psychological quality of
a play to case history developments within individual characters. Motivation can be "shared" or distributed, with one
role displaying analogy to another, and all roles contrib-
uting to a thematic unity based upon a dominant and consistent psychological principle. That a state of mind pre-

---

[6] Mr. Elliott points to a "coalescing" of the Iago and Othello roles in
III.iii (*Flaming Minister*, pp. 126, 137). But he predicates this upon a
previously developed shallowness of Othello's self-centered love (pp.
63, 67, 125–26), a quality I cannot believe is dramatically present before
III.iii.

viously established in Iago is in III.iii assumed by Othello, and that the audience accepts this because it is consistent with the play's psychological mood, is no more surprising in good dramatic art than the supplementing of Macbeth's state of mind by that of Lady Macbeth, or of Bolingbroke's by that of Northumberland.[7] So far as motivation is concerned, such pairs of characters move like binary or double stars revolving about a common axis within a gravitational field. The phenomenon is as common in nature as it is in art but seems to excite uneasiness only in the latter.

II

Traditionally, the motivation of Othello has been thought to end with his fall in III.iii, and interpreters of the play have seldom assumed that the psychological growth of his role continues through five acts. Another dramatist might have ended the matter with Cassio's beard wiped by the handkerchief, but Shakespeare chooses to begin at this point a last phase of Othello's commitment to Pride, a phase marked throughout by ritual dedication. Very infrequently have symbolic materials been used with greater meaning or with more regard for the requirements of drama.

As the strawberry-spotted handkerchief ends Othello's doubt, Shakespeare begins the second half of the tragedy in a changed key. From the point of Othello's near-attack

[7] This should not be confused with theories of one character as the alter ego of another. These are plausible, and supplement rather than conflict with the present interpretation. Another supplementary principle is also applicable here. Kenneth Burke suggests that "Iago's *ignoble* suspicions by contrast make Othello's suspicions seem *more noble*" (italics his), and observes that Shakespeare "in his way" is using James's reflector principle. "*Othello:* an Essay to Illustrate a Method," *Hudson Review,* IV (1951), 188–89.

upon Iago (lines 368–374) the temptation scene approaches realism in its dialogue of anger and suppressed violence, but some twenty lines from the end Othello subsides ominously into a formal style:

> Like to the Pontic Sea,
> Whose icy current and compulsive course
> Ne'er feels retiring ebb but keeps due on
> To the Propontic and the Hellespont,
> Even so my bloody thoughts with violent pace,
> Shall ne'er look back, ne'er ebb to humble love. . . .

The imagery first expresses hard resolve moving not impulsively but deliberately—"due on"—a tide of Nemesis, depersonalized and immense. Verse rhythms, moreover, carry the same quality. But the Homeric simile then shows a contradiction which suggests Othello's, so that a stock poetic device can be said to reveal character.[8] The initial images with their expression of slow steadiness are suddenly modified by the traditional "so" comparison which completes the figure: "Like to the Pontic sea . . ." it has begun; "Even so," it concludes, "my bloody thoughts with violent pace . . ." Blood, violence, haste thus follow stately tidal motion, but the effect is kept momentary by immediate restatement of the tidal figure; the passage ends: "Shall ne'er look back, ne'er ebb to humble love."

Lest this reading of the Pontic Sea lines be thought conjectural, I may say that my general argument does not de-

---

[8] Mr. Elliott notes sensitively the contraries of tidal motion and bloody violence in these lines, as well as their revelation of an ambiguity in Othello, but he is not concerned with a dramatic "break" in Othello's transition from one contrary to the other (*Flaming Minister*, p. 138). My emphasis is upon this break as a prelude to ensuing episodes in which stately ceremony will be destroyed by upsurging violence.

pend upon it.[9] I do not wish, however, to minimize it, for it is supported by a passage which follows the one in question. If we can agree that the long simile calls for an actor's break from calm to anger at the "even so" point, we shall find that suggestion of unstable motive by "unstable metaphor" is supplemented by dialogue and action which appear directly afterward. Ceremonialized calm begins again with Othello kneeling:

> Now by yond marble heaven,
> In the due reverence of a sacred vow
> I here engage my words.

Then Iago, quickly taking his cue from Othello's mood:

> Do not rise yet.
> Witness, you ever-burning lights above,
> You elements that clip us round about,
> Witness that here Iago doth give up
> The execution of his wit, hands, heart,
> To wrong'd Othello's service!

This is followed by Othello's almost stilted: "I greet thy love,/ Not with vain thanks, but with acceptance bounteous," a deliberative line followed, as before, by an immediate breakthrough to violent haste: "And will upon the instant put thee to 't:/ Within these three days let me hear thee say/ That Cassio's not alive." At this impulsive breach of rite Iago maintains ceremony briefly with his formal "My friend is dead," and provocatively adds, "But let her live." Here the ritual containment ends; what had been a dedication under heaven and the ever-burning stars, a solemn judg-

---

[9] My interpretation in Part II of this chapter is based upon Othello's formal or ritual phase which begins at this point; it is independent of any specific reading of the Pontic Sea passage.

ment passed upon two offenders, is broken by "Damn her, lewd minx! O, damn her! damn her!/ . . . I will withdraw/ To furnish me with some swift means of death/ For the fair devil." The ritual kneeling and intonation have expressed judicial poise and purified motive just as did the tidal figure in the earlier passage. And as the Pontic Sea image was negated by the "violent pace" comparison which arose from it, so is the kneeling ceremony destroyed by Othello's outcry which comes like a shout in church.

In the remainder of *Othello* we shall find clear development of the character conflict and moral crisis introduced by this episode. It has begun a ceremonial course of action in which Othello, assisted by Iago, invokes the light of heaven as a purifying symbol, and transmutes vengeance into even-handed justice. The dramatist's point of view is ironical: he does not, of course, imply that ritual is evil in itself, but he bases the rest of his tragedy upon subjective delusion fortified by objective ceremony. Personalized violence seeks to become impersonal action. As Shakespeare presents them, Othello's rites not only reinforce error but at the moment of performance contradict their own validity. I have tried to show how this simultaneous cleansing and contamination underlies the tragedy of Brutus; its function in *Othello* is just as significant and more pointed.

We have seen that the ritual tone at the end of III.iii is twice broken by Othello's violence of response. At the next stage of his tragedy another deliberative mood ends in similar contradiction; in IV.i at the great line, "But yet the pity of it, Iago! . . . the pity of it, Iago!" Othello, needled, again destroys the sublimity he has evoked: "I will chop her into messes. Cuckold me!" Once more he moves with violence and pace: "Get me some poison, Iago; this night . . . This night, Iago." Now, however, a return to ceremony, to symbolic action, succeeds the violence. Iago's line, "Do not do it with poison; strangle her in her bed, even the bed she hath contaminated," brings Othello's reply: "Good, good; the justice of it pleases; very good."

Symbolic justice has emerged, and the next scene begins appropriately with examination of the criminal. For this purpose Othello invents a strange mock ceremony. Scene: a brothel. Characters: Desdemona, the whore; Emilia, the proprietress; Othello, the patron—the lines which suddenly set the stage are well known. The scene, however, quickly changes as Othello's perverse imagination transforms the cast into a magistrate, a criminal, and a witness. The opening lines suggest the transcript of a court record:

> *Othello.* You have seen nothing then?
> *Emilia.* Nor even heard, nor ever did suspect. . . .
> *Othello.* What, did they never whisper?
> *Emilia.*   Never, my lord.
> *Othello.* Nor send you out o' th' way?
> *Emilia.* Never.

The stylized cross-examination continues with Desdemona's appearance:

> *Othello.*   Pray, chuck, come hither.
> *Desdemona.* What is your pleasure?
> *Othello.*   Let me see your eyes;
>   Look in my face.

And the tone of official inquiry is sustained:

> *Othello.* Are you not a strumpet?
> Desdemona.   No, as I am a Christian. . . .
> *Othello.* What, not a whore?

Desdemona.   No, as I shall be sav'd.
Othello. Is't possible?
Desdemona. O, Heaven forgive us!
Othello.   I cry you mercy, then.
   I took you for that cunning whore of Venice
   That married with Othello.

This "ceremony" differs pointedly, of course, from the ritual oath of III.iii and the coming "sacrifice" of V.ii, but it
aptly represents Othello's growing formalism. It also provides an answer to those who question his failure to deal
frankly with Desdemona, for his egoistic secretiveness comes
forth in an interlude he has composed to express it. In its
relation to III.iii and V.ii the "brothel" scene is anti-ritual
which presents Othello in a near-parody of his new-found
role.

First, then, occurs a rite, designed to sublimate violence,
in which violence breaks the spell (III.iii); next, Iago, who
had "officiated" on the first occasion, deflects Othello from
the violence of poisoning to the path of symbolic justice
(IV.i). Appropriately following this, a travesty of judicial
ceremony is enacted in an imaginary brothel (IV.ii). These
events begin Othello's ritualized course which will end in
the sacrificial murder of V.ii.

Act IV, scene ii, however, offers more than a step in this
process; it presents the motive, reputation, which by now
has become wholly egocentric. Just after his dismissal of
Desdemona's plea for understanding, Othello takes the stage
in a soliloquy on good name: "Had they rain'd/ All kind of
sores and shames on my bare head,/ . . . I should have
found . . . / A drop of patience; but, alas, to make me/
The fixed figure for the time of scorn/ To point his slow

and moving finger at! / Yet could I bear that too, well, very well." Outward disgrace is thus bearable and the insupportable shame is yet to be expressed. It is the violation of self-esteem; concern for reputation takes the final inward turn:

> But there, where I have garner'd up my heart,
> Where either I must live or bear no life;
> The fountain from the which my current runs
> Or else dries up; to be discarded thence!
> Or keep it as a cistern for foul toads
> To knot and gender in!

Desecration of the inner "fountain" calls for vengeance which, in turn, calls for consecration lest it be unworthy of the inner light. The consecration, the ritual, becomes an enshrinement of self.

Our aim is not simply to find ceremonial episodes in *Othello* and to understand their meaning. We also need to consider the art which joins them—the design which gives them additional unity and meaning. At the end of the temptation scene a symbol appears which will accompany the ritual theme from its beginning to its final statement. In describing this process I am willing to be judged by the principle that dramatic art is a public art, that symbolic elements in it should be "there." To be significant they should be both vivid and cumulative.

Robert Heilman has noted the interesting repetition at this point in *Othello* of a light symbol.[10] With an emphasis and purpose different from his I shall relate this to the subject at hand. In III.iii, Othello kneels, calling upon "yond marble heaven" to witness his dedication, and Iago, quickly kneel-

[10] "More Fair than Black: Light and Dark in *Othello*," *Essays in Criticism*, I (October, 1951), 324-25, 333-35.

ing beside him, addresses the "ever-burning lights above."
In IV.ii, just after the "anti-ritual" or "brothel" episode, the
symbol of celestial light is again invoked, this time by the
kneeling Desdemona:

> Alas, Iago,
> What shall I do to win my lord again?
> Good friend, go to him; for, by this light of heaven
> I know not how I lost him. Here I kneel.

And in IV.iii the heavenly light token appears once more,
supported by a lively interplay of tragic and comic meaning. Desdemona has asked the worldly Emilia whether
"there be women do abuse their husbands/ In such gross
kind." This follows:

> *Emilia.* There be some such, no question.
> *Desdemona.* Wouldst thou do such a deed for all the world?
> *Emilia.* Why, would not you?
> *Desdemona.* No, by this heavenly light!
> *Emilia.* Nor I neither by this heavenly light;
>   I might do't as well i' th' dark.

Before this there has been little emphasis which would bring
the symbol into dramatic relief. It has been latent, appearing
first as Othello and Iago kneel in ceremony and then as
Desdemona kneels in an impromptu rite which declares her
fidelity. But as Emilia responds to Desdemona's second invocation of heavenly light with an engaging quip which repeats it and verbally plays upon it, the device comes into the
open; its latent state changes to an active one with emphasis
at once retrospective and immediate.

The last and conclusive appearance of the figure occurs
where we might expect it, in the murder scene itself.

Othello's final obsession is expressed wholly through the ritual theme which, in turn, is controlled by the light symbol. "Enter Othello with a light." [11] Little could be made of this stage direction if it were not immediately supported by images of heavenly light which continue the original design, and if the light Othello carries were not made prominent in later lines. The invocation, "Let me not name it to you, you chaste stars!" reintroduces celestial light as a symbol of chastity; Desdemona has twice used it in this sense, Emilia has quipped that adultery cannot flourish under it, and now Othello invokes it to express the purity he thinks he is redeeming from violation. With the chaste stars appears also the holy light which is to shine over the act of "sacrifice." In this sense the symbol pointedly recalls III.iii in which the "ever-burning" stars shone upon a consecration of violence.

And now the quenching of the light, a physical prologue to murder which promptly becomes the theme of Othello's soliloquy. With lines abounding in images of light he enters a darkness both dramatically real [12] and metaphorical:

> Put out the light, and then put out the light.
> If I quench thee, thou flaming minister,
> I can again thy former light restore,
> Should I repent me; but once put out thy light,
> Thou cunning'st pattern of excelling nature,

[11] First Quarto prescribes this entry; Othello's actual carrying of the light, however, is supplemental, not necessary, to my interpretation, since lines 7 ff. stress the light symbol and imply the presence of a light upon the stage.

[12] The first part of the invocation, "If I quench thee, thou flaming minister," suggests the extinguishing of a light which Othello is carrying. On Shakespeare's stage, of course, something "representing" a light might have been used.

> I know not where is that Promethean heat
> That can thy light relume.

Obsession has become ultimate: Othello's ritualized logic is unerring, but his delusion is complete.

The murder as ritual is more than a continuation of the light symbol, for the theme of ceremonial justice also reappears. Act III, scene iii has echoed with "prove," "proof," and "probation," and IV.ii has presented Othello in a travesty of judicial cross-examination. Act IV, scene i, moreover, has turned upon Iago's insistence that Desdemona die in the bed she has "contaminated," with Othello's rejoinder, "Good, good, the justice of it pleases." In the murder scene the line, "Oh, balmy breath that dost almost persuade/ Justice to break her sword!" is significant enough as a sequel to this but it is not usually read in the context of lines which begin the scene. Critics of Shakespeare have been greatly impressed but somehow puzzled by Othello's opening passage: "It is the cause, it is the cause, my soul . . . / It is the cause." Various readings of the key word have been offered,[13] and, of course, there is the clear suggestion (escaped by much commentary) of cause as mission or purpose, a meaning which fits the ritual theme. But there is probably a further meaning derived from the old Common Law term

[13] For earlier specimen opinions, see the *Variorum*. Kittredge and Craig link this passage with the concept of justice but not in the specific sense I suggest here. Some commentators consider "cause" to mean merely Desdemona's supposed transgression, which makes the passage disturbingly banal. John Money, however, in a recent essay on the murder scene, recognizes both the legal usage of the word, which I accept, and its meaning of dedicated mission ("Othello's 'It Is the Cause . . .' an Analysis," *Shakespeare Survey* VI, 1953, 94–105). Mr. Money, who has "undertaken this study as an actor," provides unusual insight into the formalized, incantatory quality of Othello's opening passage and discusses its ironical implications.

"cause" which connoted a legal process. Perhaps this sense of the word combines with the more general one of dedicated mission and serves to connect the "cause" passage with Othello's line on the sword of justice.

Othello's ritual in the murder scene is an elaborate one. In addition to casting himself as light-bearer and minister of Justice, he suggests the role of priest: "Have you pray'd tonight, Desdemon?/ . . . Well, do it . . . / I would not kill thy unprepared spirit;/ . . . I would not kill thy soul./ . . . Think on thy sins." And after implying the Christian office of absolution he introduces the pagan one of sacrifice:

> O perjur'd woman! thou dost stone my heart,
> And mak'st me call what I intend to do
> A murder, which I thought a sacrifice.

Othello's intended rite has been implicit throughout, but his line, "A murder, which I thought a sacrifice," defeats the intention at the moment of explicit statement. Without real awareness he tells the truth about his ritual act; once more ceremony mocks itself and its contriver. And as liturgy turns into murder, even the symbolic tone of the scene is ended by Emilia, one of Shakespeare's most naturalistic characters. Her cry, "O gull! O dolt!/ As ignorant as dirt!" brings the denouement.

Here then, under the "heavenly light," the magistrate-priest-sacrificer has performed his last rite of self-delusion. To say this is not to pass final judgment upon Othello, for few of Shakespeare's characters exceed him in ultimate self-knowledge. This knowledge will come, however, only after he advances a last claim to ceremonial honor. Lodovico becomes the accuser:

> O thou Othello, that wast once so good,
> Fall'n in the practice of a cursed slave,
> What shall be said to thee?

And Othello can only reply:

> Why anything.
> An honourable murder, if you will;
> For nought I did in hate, but all in honour.

Pathetically, defensively, now knowing what he has done, he still holds to the rite of hateless sacrifice.

There remain some eighty lines of the play, and within that space Othello gains the self-awareness which Macbeth, Hamlet, and Lear achieve much earlier. In Othello the denouement and the appearance of full tragic stature are almost simultaneous. Othello's reply to Lodovico finds him still holding to honor and its expression in unwrathful rite, so that it would be easy to say that he evolves no further, that even at the end he tries to justify the ceremony of loving bloodshed by dying "upon a kiss." Honor and rite, however, undergo change, for at his death Othello is free from the egoistic concern for reputation which drove him to the "sacrifice" of V.ii and to the ritual acts which prepared for it. In his last declaration, "Soft you; a word or two before you go," his honor is no longer a formalized defense against the inner knotting and gendering of toads; it is the quality he once showed upon facing Brabantio and the Venetian Council. "I have done the state some service and they know't./ No more of that." "Speak of me as I am; nothing extenuate,/ Nor set down aught in malice."

> Set you down this;
> And say besides, that in Aleppo once,
> Where a malignant and a turban'd Turk
> Beat a Venetian and traduc'd the state,

> I took by th' throat the circumcised dog,
> And smote him—thus.

With these lines of understatement setting forth a half-forgotten incident, pride is purged as the reputation theme appears for the last time. Killing the nameless dog who "traduc'd" the state was a vindication of Venetian good-name, and Othello's humble irony in speaking of the incident frees him from Iago's inversion of the reputation ideal.

III

Traditionally, the part played in *Othello* by Desdemona's handkerchief has often been understood as melodrama which detracts, not too seriously, from tragic "inevitability." Such an interpretation is possible only if the handkerchief is viewed merely as a plot device and ignored as a symbol.

The handkerchief makes its first appearance in the temptation scene as Desdemona seeks to bind Othello's head with it after Iago's suggestion begins to work. Othello, of course, rejects it with the line, "Your napkin is too little," which implies the irony of later events. Then in a passage which quickly follows, the napkin becomes a talisman. It was Desdemona's "first remembrance from the Moor"; Iago has sought the stealing of it "a hundred times," but Desdemona "so loves the token," Othello having "conjur'd" her to keep it, that "she reserves it evermore about her/ To kiss and talk to." Iago next introduces it to cap his mission of deception. Cassio, he declares, has wiped his beard with it, which causes Othello's paroxysm, "Arise, black vengeance from the hollow hell!" and leads, for our purposes, directly into the first episode of ritual dedication, the kneeling ceremony at the end of III.iii.

The following scene brings the expected impasse in which Desdemona is unable upon Othello's request to produce the handkerchief, and at this point Shakespeare increases its symbolic quality.

>   That handkerchief
> Did an Egyptian to my mother give;
> She was a charmer, and could almost read
> The thoughts of people. She told her, while she kept it
> 'Twould make her amiable and subdue my father
> Entirely to her love, but if she lost it,
> Or made a gift of it, my father's eye
> Should hold her loathed, and his spirits should hunt
> After new fancies.

Then as Othello adjures Desdemona to keep the napkin, for "to lose 't or giv 't away were such perdition/ As nothing else could match," he redoubles its meaning with incantation upon the magic [14] of its web, the "prophetic fury" of the sibyl who "sew'd the work," the "hallowed" worms that bred the silk, and the dye made of "mummy which the skilful/ Conserv'd of maiden's hearts." All this is followed by his demanding and redemanding of the object; three times, as Desdemona begins to intercede for Cassio, Othello stops her peremptorily with his refrain line: "The handkerchief!"

At the end of III.iv Cassio dramatically sullies the token by presenting it to Bianca, his whore. Significantly enough, it stirs her haughty jealousy which, with his comment upon her "vile guesses," forms an interlude of invidious surmise which supports the serious theme of the play. By IV.i the symbol has so grown in Othello's mind that he can exclaim, "It comes o'er my memory/ As doth the raven o'er the in-

---

[14] On the "wonder" and "magic" of the handkerchief, see further Kenneth Burke, "*Othello:* an Essay to Illustrate a Method," *Hudson Review,* IV (1951), 196–200.

fectious house." Midway in the same scene it appears three
times as a random image in the passage which precedes his
collapse, his falling "in a trance." And the succeeding lines
of IV.i center entirely upon the napkin as Iago maneuvers
Othello into listening as Cassio bickers with Bianca about it.
At Cassio's laughter over the hallowed object, Desdemona's
adultery is "confirmed," and Othello's blindness becomes
complete.

When the bitter secretiveness of the "brothel" scene
passes, the handkerchief reappears and in the remainder of
the play it is used twice, each time briefly but with great
effect. Othello's sudden remembrance of it in V.ii is the
event which ends his ritual phase and causes him, unaware
of real meaning, to describe his act for what it is:

> And mak'st me call what I intend to do
> A murder, which I thought a sacrifice.
> I saw the handkerchief.

He can state but he cannot see what the symbol does to his
course of symbolic action. After the murder he invokes it
again as a last remnant of justification:

> I saw it in his hand;
> It was a handkerchief. . . .

Then the full truth comes, and it is revealed by Emilia entirely in terms of the "antique token."

So it is clear that the handkerchief is neither a stage prop-
erty nor a symbol which is merely static. In the beginning
it signifies enduring marriage: kept by Desdemona, it means
lasting happiness; lost by her it spells ruin (III.iv.55–68).
Shortly, however, in its developing function the token
comes to represent both Desdemona's chastity and the

world of confirmatory fact, the proof or "probation" which bears "no hinge or loop." Desdemona's failure to produce it, Cassio's possession of it—these are the "facts" which prompt Othello's delusion and his recourse to symbolic certainty, to incanted thought and stylized act, as a release from the indefinite, the ambiguous, or the unknown. Here the handkerchief enters into the ritual design; just as ceremony and incantation become the equivalents of moral responsibility, so a bit of linen properly hallowed and intoned over, becomes identified with circumstantial fact.

It is unperceptive to regard Shakespeare's plan as fabulous or to infer from it that Othello is a primitive or superstitious character. Those who know symbolic thought and action to be perennially human, and who understand that all human attributes are interchangeably sound or perverse, will hardly find Othello's tragedy unrepresentative. This does not mean, of course, that the play resembles the surface of life. We scarcely have here a family-man judging his wife by her care of an object which he has made significant, and striking defensive attitudes which he may or may not know are ritualistic. But if this common situation were to be turned into a modern play, its very realism would depend upon the author's understanding of token and ritual in human behavior. If he should find a style suitable for tragedy and portray his ritual-ridden character with a formalized art, he might provide the modern equivalent of *Othello*. Symbolic drama can be the best psychological drama because symbolic behavior, now understood as central to psychology, is most readily depicted by symbolic media. An Othello so presented is the genuine semblance of an actual mind tragically bent; traditional realism or naturalism cannot equal it.

ix. "*Look, how our partner's rapt*"

THE exceptional unity of *Macbeth*
is partly based upon four themes [1]—darkness, sleep, raptness, and contradiction—which combine to give the play
much of its character. Although darkness and sleep have
long been known to play a part in *Macbeth*, neither their
extent nor their bearing upon other elements has been noted.
Their familiarity, however, makes it unnecessary to describe
them, so that definition may be confined to the two remaining themes. Raptness (Banquo's word) is present in forms
which vary from simple abstraction to near-hypnosis. Contradiction is of two kinds: there is the outright expression
of it in "fair is foul and foul is fair," or "nothing is but what
is not," and there is its appearance simply as inverted nature,
exemplified by the beards of the weird sisters or by Duncan's
horses which eat each other. In Elizabethan tradition, however, the two forms of contradiction were one in that they
both implied chaos and overturned hierarchy. All four
themes, incidentally, were conventional,[2] and my purpose

[1] These are called themes for want of a better term. See the introductory
chapter. Other themes, of course, are present; that of "blood," for example,
is so prevalent that its association with any discoverable pattern is to be
assumed.

[2] Several studies recognize this. Paul V. Kreider furnishes a collection
of passages on sleep (*Repetition in Shakespeare's Plays*, Princeton, 1941,

here as elsewhere is not so much to "discover" materials as to show with what skill they are amplified, varied, and unified to an end.

These themes are not confined to poetic statement; they also appear as drama, and thus become clear and direct with no loss of suggestive quality: darkness is a constant setting for the action; sleep is physically murdered by Macbeth who then "shall sleep no more"; raptness is rendered as action before the murder, during it, and afterward (the sleepwalking scene); and contradiction is a key to the tragic reversal. The themes as drama, moreover, blend with their poetic equivalents.

Such a unity of design would lack importance if it did not contribute to an interpretation of the play, and for the sake of clarity I shall suggest the interpretation here. *Macbeth* is based upon the familiar tragic motive of sin and self-destruction which are compulsive.[3] The surrender to the witches is a surrender to "instruments of darkness," to "secret, black, and midnight hags," and with it appears

---

pp. 178–93). In an article which shortly followed mine (*Shakespeare Quarterly*, Oct., 1953, pp. 167–90) Margaret D. Burrell discusses passages of paradox and inversion ("Macbeth: a Study in Paradox," *Shakespeare Jahrbuch*, XC, 1954, 167–90). On the protean, dark, and sleepless world of *Macbeth*, see also Mark Van Doren's excellent discussion in his *Shakespeare* (New York, 1939). For an unusual recognition of the motifs of light and darkness, see Roy Walker, *The Time Is Free* (London, 1949), *passim*.

[3] The stressing of compulsion does not mean, of course, that *Macbeth* is a tragedy of clinical neurosis. Nor is the play a clear tragedy of fate, for although Macbeth's conduct after his traffic with the witches may be determined, his early submission to them can be viewed as an act of free will. On this difficult question note, however, the contrast between Macbeth, who is spellbound from the moment of encounter with the supernatural, and Hamlet, who exhibits deliberate free choice in deciding whether the Ghost is "a spirit of health or goblin damned." Although unorthodox, the concept of predestined sin was scarcely unfamiliar in sixteenth-century doctrinal conflict.

Macbeth's raptness, an obsessive state which implies contradiction, since from its onset "nothing is but what is not." Contradiction within raptness now governs both character and play, as a great rhetoric of conscience accompanies the almost hypnotic murder of sleep.[4] And as obsession under the spell of darkness leads to added murder—violence dedicated to peace and sleep—the ultimate contradiction occurs. Macbeth's abstraction gives way to awareness of reality, while Lady Macbeth's early command of pseudo-reality advances into the guilty raptness of walking sleep.

The themes of darkness and contradiction are presented in the opening incantation scene. "When shall we three meet again/ In thunder, lightning, or in rain?" are lines which suggest the gloom of storm; they are succeeded by "When the battle's lost and won," an assertion of contradiction, and are reinforced immediately with another connotation of darkness, "That will be ere the set of sun." This is followed five lines later with the contradiction of "Fair is foul, and foul is fair," and the last line of the short scene then reverts to cloudiness: "Hover through the fog and filthy air." Two themes are thus begun within twelve opening lines. And although the ensuing scene of the bleeding messenger is one of mechanical exposition, the effects of darkness and contradiction are not allowed to lapse:

> As whence the sun 'gins his reflection
> Shipwrecking storms and direful thunders break,
> So from that spring whence comfort seem'd to come
> Discomfort swells.

[4] For a relationship between Macbeth's moral utterance and his commitment to evil, see Arnold Stein, "Macbeth and Word-magic," *Sewanee Review*, Spring, 1951, pp. 271–84.

This introduction to the uneasy turn of battle stresses the blackness of storm proceeding from sunlight, and moves from the simile itself into outright statement of the inversion it represents. Darkness and contradiction are combined in one figure.

The second incantation of the witches which opens scene iii is significant because the curse pronounced upon the sailor, "master o' the Tiger," is the fate which Macbeth himself will suffer:

> Sleep shall neither night nor day
> Hang upon his pent-house lid;
> He shall live a man forbid.
> Weary sev'nights nine times nine
> Shall he dwindle, peak, and pine.
> Though his bark cannot be lost,
> Yet it shall be tempest-tost.

This thematic passage introduces the murdered sleep of later events, and continues the previous design; it maintains the setting of night, and ends in a contradiction image of the loss-threatened bark which can never be lost. Then, as the "charm's wound up," the line, "So foul and fair a day I have not seen," echoes the fair-foul contradiction which closed scene i. Upon appearance of the witches this is succeeded and augmented by symbols of inverted nature: unearthly inhabitants of earth and bearded women. Now, as the triple prophecy of Macbeth's fortune is concluded, the raptness theme is introduced by Banquo: "My noble partner/ You greet with present grace and great prediction/ . . . That he seems rapt withal," which is echoed toward the end of the scene with "Look, how our partner's rapt," and two scenes later with the line from Macbeth's letter, "Whiles I stood rapt in the wonder of it. . . ."

Scene iii is thus one of motivation, for the two moods which will lend character to Macbeth are both presented. His abstraction which will lead to murder appears through Banquo's lines, and the ruined sleep which will follow his act is suggested by the witch's curse upon the sailor. Emphasis of motive comes most strongly, however, from Macbeth himself in a passage which avows the rapt state Banquo has described, and does so in the now familiar terms of contradiction. Raptness is expressed here through the "suggestion/ Whose horrid image doth unfix my hair . . ." and the "thought" which "shakes so my single state of man that function/ Is smother'd in surmise. . . ." But the passage has begun upon a note of contradiction expressed in "This supernatural soliciting/ Cannot be ill, cannot be good . . . ," and it ends with the same theme: "and nothing is/ But what is not." More, the entire soliloquy has been prefaced by Banquo who has evoked another of the themes: "The instruments of darkness tell us truths,/ Win us with honest trifles. . . ."

Act I, scene iii is now concluded with Macbeth's return from the world of obsession: "Give me your favour; my dull brain was wrought/ With things forgotten." The return, however, is momentary, for as Duncan in the ensuing scene confirms Macbeth's title of Cawdor, the mood recurs, and again darkness combines with abstracted compulsion:

> Stars, hide your fires;
> Let not light see my black and deep desires;
> The eye wink at the hand; yet let that be
> Which the eye fears, when it is done, to see.

While there is a suggestion of contradiction here, actual emphasis of it occurs twenty lines later in scene v after Lady Macbeth has read the letter. Here her description of Mac-

beth plays cumulatively upon the theme in such lines as "Art
not without ambition, but without/ The illness should attend it," or "Wouldst not play false,/ And yet wouldst
wrongly win," or "And that which rather thou dost fear to
do/ Than wishest should be undone."

At this point the messenger's entry with news of Duncan
releases the pattern in augmented form. Night and blackness abound: "The King comes here tonight"—"The raven
himself is hoarse/ That croaks the fatal entrance of Duncan . . ."—"Come, thick night,/ And pall thee in the dun-
nest smoke of hell/ . . . Nor heaven peep through the
blanket of the dark . . ."—"Duncan comes here tonight"—
"O, never/ Shall sun that morrow see"—and the culmina-
tion of planned evil, again in terms of night:

> . . . you shall put
> This night's great business into my dispatch,
> Which shall to all our nights and days to come
> Give solely sovereign sway and masterdom.

Notable also is the one clear reference to murder; it combines darkness with blind raptness: "Come thick night . . ./
That my keen knife see not the wound it makes. . . ." Finally, contradiction joins the other themes in figures of inverted nature: "Come, you spirits/ . . . unsex me here,
. . . Come to my woman's breasts,/ And take my milk for
gall. . . ." After this mingling in I.v of abstraction and violated nature with the blackness of night, there is no need
to comment upon the irony of Duncan's line from the next
brief scene, "Fair and noble hostess,/ We are your guest tonight."

The opening of I.vii asserts contradiction again in the
form of that which is done, yet never is to be finished: "If

it were done when 'tis done. . . ." The thought is then expanded in a passage which is ultimate, for a turn of phrase,
"that but this blow/ Might be the be-all and the end-all
here . . . ," expresses all of Macbeth's struggle for rest in
a present which can offer nothing but a guilty past and a
fear-ridden future. It is partly because the tragedy is built
around this irony that the pattern of inversion in *Macbeth*
is so telling. It would even be possible to say that the whole
play is an extended metaphor of contradiction but I am
afraid that this would invoke the old platitude that tragedy
involves irony, as well as a newer one that paradox, like
ripeness, is all. Not all tragedy, however, involves schematic
play upon contradiction in skillful combination with other
themes, and it is this characteristic which I desire to em-
phasize.

"If it were done when 'tis done, then 'twere well/ It were
done quickly." Done quickly it is; in the speed of the doing
Shakespeare shows himself the tested dramatist, for he rests
his motivation less upon Macbeth's psychological traits than
upon a pervasive quality of the play itself. He thus employs
a method suited to concentrated movement, but the method
is not one merely of combining action with a static "atmos-
phere." This will become clear as we note the extraordinary
merging of theme and action which gives the thematic or
motivating background a directness required by the stage
but retains its poetic indirection. An example of this appears
in the remainder of I.vii. In lines following "If it were done
when 'tis done" Macbeth withdraws from raptness, and in
one of the strongest passages of the play attempts moral
judgment with the speech beginning, "He's here in double
trust," which invokes the virtues of Duncan—angels, plead-

ing "trumpet-tongued, against/ The deep damnation of his taking-off." Then the decision:

> We will proceed no further in this business.
> He hath honour'd me of late; and I have bought
> Golden opinions from all sorts of people,
> Which would be worn now in their newest gloss,
> Not cast aside so soon.

Lady Macbeth's attack upon her husband's conscience then resolves a dramatic clash which ends in the unconscious irony of "Bring forth men-children only. . . ." Significantly, this turn of event is secured by lines which restate under heavy stress the two themes of sleep and raptness. Consciousness must abdicate while murder is done: "When Duncan is asleep" Lady Macbeth will so tend his chamberlains,

> That memory, the warder of the brain,
> Shall be a fume, and the receipt of reason
> A limbeck only. When in swinish sleep
> Their drenched natures lie as in a death,
> What cannot you and I perform upon
> Th' unguarded Duncan?

And as her thought is echoed in Macbeth's own words: "When we have mark'd with blood those sleepy two/ Of his own chamber . . . ," the world of night, sleep, and insensate drift has been reasserted in combination with vivid outward conflict.

With the opening of Act II movement is accelerated, but Shakespeare intensifies the presence of darkness and sleep: "How goes the night . . . ?"—"The moon is down . . ." —"There's husbandry in heaven;/ Their candles are all out" —"A heavy summons lies like lead upon me,/ And yet I would not sleep"—"The king's a-bed"—"Good repose the while"—"Get thee to bed." Then as the symbolic dagger appears, another theme comes physically upon the stage as the vision draws Macbeth abstractedly toward the murder chamber to an accompaniment of lines which express his raptness and blend with it the elements of night and sleep:

> Thou marshall'st me the way that I was going,
> And such an instrument I was to use.
> Mine eyes are made the fools o' the other senses
> Or else worth all the rest. . . .
>   Now o'er the one half-world
> Nature seems dead, and wicked dreams abuse
> The curtain'd sleep. Witchcraft celebrates
> Pale Hecate's offerings, and wither'd Murder,
> Alarum'd by his sentinel, the wolf,
> Whose howl's his watch, thus with his stealthy pace,
> With Tarquin's ravishing strides, towards his design
> Moves like a ghost. Thou sure and firm set earth,
> Hear not my steps, which way they walk. . . .
> I go, and it is done; the bell invites me.
> Hear it not, Duncan; for it is a knell
> That summons thee to heaven or to hell.

In examining the last of Act I and the first of Act II we have traced the way in which undercurrents of poetic theme begin to combine with outward action: the note of contradiction in "If it were done when 'tis done," which opened I.vii, led to a moral resurgence which carried Macbeth into sudden conflict with his temptress; his conscience was enveloped and deadened, however, by Lady Macbeth's evocation of murder presided over by drugged sleep. At this, movement toward the murder began with a setting established in cumulative terms of sleep and night. And with Macbeth's approach to the chamber of Duncan, raptness took dramatic form in his actual drift across the stage and the lines on the dagger which accompanied it.

We have now come to the murder scene, and it is here that underlying theme and external action meet in climactic unity. As figures of night and darkness preside, the killing of Duncan is made physically the murder of sleep ("Had he not resembled/ My father as he slept, I had done 't"), a fusion of theme with action which leads to the great passage ending "Glamis hath murder'd sleep . . ./ Macbeth shall sleep no more." And here raptness again becomes action as Macbeth enters bearing obliviously the incriminating daggers. Summary or quotation can convey neither his "brainsickly" isolation nor Lady Macbeth's attempts to break through the barrier: "Be not lost so poorly in your thoughts." The scene must be read entire to sense the magnitude of the effect.

No less prominent is a translation into dramatic terms of the remaining theme. The drunken porter is no longer excluded from Shakespeare's creations, but all arguments for readmitting him to *Macbeth* are whimsically confirmed when we realize that he is the perfect embodiment of contradiction. Lear's fool is scarcely more appropriate than he as the spokesman of a world in which *non-sequitur* has final relevance because degree and a stable chain of being have been destroyed.[5] "Knock, knock"—images of contradiction spill upon the scene: the farmer "that hanged himself

[5] But there is a difference. The theme of *non-sequitur* in *Lear* usually appears as logic which mocks because it is so "logical"; the same theme in *Macbeth* is expressed in the many instances we have noted by inversion of logic which, although it secures a similar effect, is fundamentally the opposite of the *reductio ad absurdum* in *Lear*.

On logical antithesis as a quality of the porter scene which identifies it with the play, see Kenneth Muir's brief comment in the New Arden edition of *Macbeth* (London, 1951), p. xxxiii and note.

on th' expectation of plenty"; the equivocator who "could swear in both the scales against either scale . . ." and whose treason for God's sake could not equivocate him into heaven; lechery which drink "provokes and unprovokes"— "It makes him and it mars him; it sets him on, and it takes him off; it persuades him, and disheartens him; makes him stand to, and not stand to. . . ." Truly, nothing is but what is not. With this tour de force the murder scenes are complete in their stressing of previously set themes; darkness has been the setting, Duncan has become the stage presence of sleep, and Macbeth himself has enacted the quality of raptness. Through the porter Shakespeare dramatizes the fourth element of contradiction.

"In conclusion, equivocates him in a sleep . . ."—the porter thus ends his speech, and sleep with night now strangely prevails in the hectic scene of discovery. Inquiries which precede the disclosure come in ironic terms of disturbed slumber: "Is thy Master stirring?/ Our knocking has awak'd him."—"Is the King stirring . . . ?" The setting of darkness is reestablished: "The night has been unruly. . . . The obscure bird/ Clamour'd the livelong night." When mood and suspense are secured in this way, the murder is suddenly revealed in Macduff's passage beginning "Confusion now hath made his masterpiece." Here the hue and cry combines sleep, which is equated with death, and raptness represented by spirits who rise and walk.

> Malcolm! awake!
> Shake off this downy sleep, death's counterfeit,
> And look on death itself! Up, up, and see . . .
> As from your graves rise up, and walk like sprites,
> To countenance this horror!

The unmasking of murder within the precincts of sleep is finally capped by Lady Macbeth's "What's the business,/ That such a hideous trumpet calls to parley/ The sleepers of the house?"

Act II, scene iv is a choric scene which "points the way" as clearly as the episode of the gardeners in *Richard II;* Ross and a prophetic Old Man meet for the sole purpose of commenting upon what has happened, and the burden of their speech is the contradiction of nature so frequent in *Macbeth* and in lesser contemporary accounts of rebellion and regicide. From their lines we learn that Duncan's death has been accompanied by a falcon "hawk'd at" by a mousing owl, together with the king's horses, "turn'd wild in nature," which have so overthrown the law of kind that "they eat each other." And as Macduff brings news that Malcolm and Donalbain are suspected of the murder, Ross, continuing his role, cries out, " 'Gainst nature still." These expressions of inverted "degree" are hackneyed enough, but there is a revealing quality in Shakespeare's manner of beginning and concluding them. They are introduced in Ross's passage which joins two previous themes by expressing contradiction through imagery of night:

> By the clock 'tis day,
> And yet dark night strangles the travelling lamp.
> Is't night's predominance or the day's shame
> That darkness does the face of earth entomb,
> When living light should kiss it?

After starting the scene in this way, Shakespeare ends it with another statement of contradiction in the Old Man's blessing:

> God's benison go with you; and with those
> That would make good of bad, and friends of foes!

In its unobtrusive way, this brief scene is fundamental.[6] It
is a choric piece which appears at the point between culmi-
nation of the murder and movement toward expiation by
the murderer. Its meaning is drawn from the world of inverted nature and thus, appropriately, it is tied to past action
and future event by two assertions of contradiction, one
at the beginning and the other at the end. The passage beginning the scene expresses destructive inversion in multiple
terms of the night theme which has so prominently governed the rising action; the passage ending it invokes re-
storative inversion through the Old Man's sanctification of
those who are about to institute the falling action.

Act III continues the course of murder in which "returning were as tedious as go o'er," and the onslaught upon
Banquo is accompanied by the same thematic design which
gave meaning to Acts I and II. In the first scene tragic
irony is lent to Banquo's departure by his announcement
of it in terms of darkness:

> Go not my horse the better,
> I must become a borrower of the night
> For a dark hour or twain,

which is strengthened by Macbeth's reply, "Hie you to
horse; adieu,/ Till you return at night." The scene now
presents Macbeth and the two murderers, and in the soliloquy which ends it the same theme takes prominence: "for't

---

[6] It is interesting that Mr. G. B. Harrison in his recent treatment of
Macbeth finds the scene just discussed to be the work of a "collaborator
or hack": "Neither the rhythms nor the forced and fantastic image of dark
Night strangling a travelling lamp are in the manner of Shakespeare, at
least not of Shakespeare mature and sober." *Shakespeare's Tragedies* (London, 1950), p. 186. Sober or not, Shakespeare manages here to combine
themes which have previously governed the play and which will continue
to govern it. As for Mr. Harrison's hack-collaborator, he seems at least
to have been well briefed on the themes of contradiction and darkness.

must be done tonight/. . . . Banquo, thy soul's flight,/ If
it find heaven, must find it out tonight." Should this linkage of impending murder with the theme of darkness seem
tenuous, a reference forward to the commentary of scene
vi will strengthen it. There Banquo's death is directly
ascribed to traffic with night:

> The gracious Duncan
> Was pitied of Macbeth; marry, he was dead.
> And the right-valiant Banquo walk'd too late. . . .

And lest the allusion escape as casual, it is immediately repeated:

> Whom [Banquo], you may say, if't please you, Fleance
> killed,
> For Fleance fled; men must not walk too late.

If after this reference ahead, we now return to Act III,
scene ii, there will be found a major rendering of the night-
spell which dooms Banquo. Preceding it, however, the note
of contradiction occurs in Lady Macbeth's "Naught's had,
all's spent,/ Where our desire is got without content," and
murdered sleep arises in redoubled irony with "Duncan is
in his grave;/ After life's fitful fever he sleeps well." Then
appears the theme of darkness; the passage begins:

> Ere the bat hath flown
> His cloister'd flight, ere to black Hecate's summons
> The shard-borne beetle with his drowsy hums
> Hath rung night's yawning peal. . . .

And as the night imagery multiplies it evolves to raptness
equalling hypnosis: first made sightless by the invocation to
darkness, "pitiful day," the symbol of conscience, is made
"to droop and drowse."

> Come seeling night,
> Scarf up the tender eye of pitiful day,
> And with thy bloody and invisible hand
> Cancel and tear to pieces that great bond
> Which keeps me pale! Light thickens and the crow
> Makes wing to the rooky wood;
> Good things of day begin to droop and drowse,
> Whiles night's black agents to their preys do rouse.
> Thou marvell'st at my words.

It is clear, moreover, that the sleep-raptness note in this address to night also takes auditory form: "summons," "hums," "yawning," "drowse," "rouse" transmit it in the manner of Spenser's *m, n,* and *z* sounds in the Cave of Morpheus episode.

The prelude to Banquo's murder thus reproduces and intensifies the setting which accompanied the murder of Duncan. All of the previous themes are repeated, and they appear in such concentrated suspension that the burst of action in III.iii occurs as a sudden liberation of evil: in some twenty lines the death of Banquo is accomplished, just as the killing of Duncan was carried out in a quick scene which followed similar dramatic preparation. But in this kinetic release darkness can still accompany the action and, in fact, strike the climax: "The west yet glimmers . . ." —"Give us a light there!"—"A light, a light!" And as Banquo dies, the Third Murderer: "Who did strike out the light?"

After Banquo's ghost has walked, Macbeth makes his last trial for the certainty, the sleep, which he has lost irrevocably. In IV.i his second visit to the witches will yield the false prophecy of safety, and as the creatures prepare for his coming their incantation draws appreciably upon imagery of darkness: "wool of bat," "owlet's wing," "root of hemlock digg'd i' th' dark," "slips of yew/ Sliver'd in the moon's eclipse"—all of this provides the setting for Macbeth's entry line, "How now, you secret, black, and midnight hags!" which recalls Banquo's earlier allusion to the witches as "instruments of darkness." With this greeting Macbeth submits himself finally to the world of night and draws from it the tragic afflatus which will collapse when Birnam Wood comes to Dunsinane.

But if Macbeth's drawing of solace from the witches has been his final entry into the dark, so has Lady Macbeth's enduring of torment become the last stage of her traffic with night. Hell here is not fiery, but "murky." Primarily, of course, the sleepwalking scene enacts the raptness or near-hypnosis which has sustained so much of the play. The scene is more, however, than a presentation of this single theme; it offers in some form all of the others—sleep, darkness, contradiction—and thus preserves the unified design. Prior to this scene, raptness has not always been associated with sleep, nor do the two imply each other, but here, from the nature of Lady Macbeth's affliction, they appear in combination. The quality of darkness is, of course, immediately to be linked with sleepwalking, but Shakespeare is not content with the obvious association; he specifically introduces fear of night as a motive: "How came she by that light?/ . . . She has light by her continually; 'tis her command." And the line "Hell is murky!" suggests more than random combination. Finally, contradiction in its traditional form appears in a description by the Doctor of sleepwalking as "a great perturbation in nature." It is present, however, in a sense far more pervasive than this, for

Lady Macbeth's last scene is the terminus of a great inversion which has been shaping itself throughout the play. In the opening action Macbeth was almost the somnambulist, so stricken was he by prophecy that he drifted toward and through the murder of Duncan in rapt isolation; and also in the beginning it was Lady Macbeth who exhibited supremely the hyperconsciousness, the "outside" directive force which controlled the movements of her husband's abstracted state. From thence, however, the major reversal begins; it is Macbeth who becomes the active, conscious force and his wife who lapses into semiconscious passivity: "Be innocent of the knowledge, dearest chuck,/ Till thou applaud the deed"—through this stage of the inversion she passes, as her husband's pragmatic awareness grows, until in the sleepwalking scene she assumes his former role of absent, lonely obsession. So at this stage of the play she has herself become a symbol of contradiction; in a world where fair is foul and foul is fair, where the battle's lost and won, where storms issue from sunlight and night falls by day, the watchful puppeteer has turned into the unseeing puppet. And this transformation has been concluded in a setting of darkness, sleep, and raptness which preserves the prevailing context of themes.

"Tomorrow, and tomorrow, and tomorrow" marks the stage at which Macbeth's inner defeat becomes final. Save for the missing note of sleep, this episode also is carried by themes which have supplemented one another throughout and which have so unified action, character, and mood. Here, in the lighting of fools to dusty death, is connoted the scene of Macbeth led raptly by the "air-drawn dagger" and, as well, the spectacle of Lady Macbeth with her

light amidst the darkness of walking sleep. Life, the "walking shadow," suggests further this abstracted movement.
In the strut and fret of the player, emphasis without sense,
comes the note of contradiction which is struck again in
the idiot's tale, "signifying nothing." Once more the fatal
insight, the function-smothering surmise in terms of contradictory being; again "nothing is but what is not." Lastly,
the symbol of darkness persists in "Out, out, brief candle,"
and a continuation of the night theme is allowed to end the
inner tragedy after the soliloquy is finished. Macbeth, no
longer responsive even to the "night-shriek," can now say
"I gin to be aweary of the sun. . . ."

x. "*The nobleness of life*"

IN G. B. Shaw's preface to *Three Plays for Puritans* there is a spirited disposition of *Antony and Cleopatra* which is both well remembered and often misunderstood.

The very name of Cleopatra suggests at once a tragedy of Circe, with the horrible difference that whereas the ancient myth rightly represents Circe as turning heroes into hogs, the modern romantic convention would represent her as turning hogs into heroes. Shakespear's *Antony and Cleopatra* must needs be as intolerable to the true Puritan as it is vaguely distressing to the ordinary healthy citizen, because, after giving a faithful picture of the soldier broken down by debauchery, and the typical wanton in whose arms such men perish, Shakespear finally strains all his huge command of rhetoric and stage pathos to give a theatrical sublimity to the wretched end of the business, and to persuade foolish spectators that the world was well lost by the twain. Such falsehood is not to be borne except by the real Cleopatras and Antonys (they are to be found in every public house) who would no doubt be glad enough to be transfigured by some poet as immortal lovers. Woe to the poet who stoops to such folly! The lot of the man who sees life truly and thinks about it romantically is Despair. . . .

Shaw continues with "a technical objection to making sexual infatuation a tragic theme." Experience shows that it should be assigned, perhaps not eagerly, to forms other than tragedy:

Let realism have its demonstration, comedy its criticism, or even bawdry its horselaugh at the expense of sexual infatuation, if it must; but to ask us to subject our souls to its ruinous glamor, to worship it, deify it, and imply that it alone makes our life worth living, is nothing but folly gone mad erotically— a thing compared to which Falstaff's unbeglamored drinking and drabbing is respectable and rightminded.[1]

The rhetoric here may be Victorian but, contrary to most of Shaw's critics, it is not framed to deny sexual infatuation a place in literature; rather, it merely asks that the passion remain "unbeglamored." Allow realism and comedy to treat the subject, but be mature enough to resist the glow which tragedy often casts upon it and other forms of egoistic obsession. Very few will deny that if Shakespeare's art actually expresses moral nihilism on a sentimental plane, it is at least a misapplied art. And there is no doubt that many have found a lush irresponsibility in *Antony and Cleopatra;* some have artlessly rejoiced in it and some, like Shaw, have rejected it. Is the play open to his criticism? Despite a touch of melodrama, the charge is a serious and considered one which is still current.[2] The answer to it can-

[1] This quotation and the one which precedes it are from "Better than Shakespear," in *The Collected Works of Bernard Shaw* (New York, 1930), Vol. IX, pp. xxx–xxxii. Reprinted by permission of the Public Trustee and the Society of Authors, London.

[2] Its currency is best seen in recent and repeated attempts to meet the issues it raises. Willard Farnham shows historically that the paradox of tragic greatness and intensified flaw became increasingly prominent in Shakespeare's last tragedies and those of his Jacobean contemporaries (*Shakespeare's Tragic Frontier,* Berkeley, Calif., 1950). J. F. Danby points to a dialectic within the play in which no single attitude, such as "autotoxic exaltation," becomes dominant or controlling. (*Poets on Fortune's Hill,* London, 1952, pp. 128–51.) See also the comment on Mr.

not lie in a reminder that Elizabethans would disagree, or that sexual infatuation is a part of "life," or that Shakespeare redeems Antony by giving him true Roman stature. All such replies ignore the question; in this play the spell of Circe is either beglamored or it is not.

In the first part of this chapter I hope to show that Shakespeare did not "see life truly and think about it romantically," and that there is no meretricious sublimity cast even over the ending of *Antony and Cleopatra*. Instead, it is engagingly satirical throughout, but it remains great tragedy because the satire is combined effectively with other qualities. It is interesting that Shakespeare seems to have anticipated the problem of sexual infatuation as a tragic theme by actually posing the question as a theme within his play. Conventional "romantic" tragedy, with its concepts of stature-in-degradation, flaw, and soulful catastrophe, becomes an issue among the characters very early in the action. Disposition of the issue occurs, moreover, at the very place in which Shaw thought that satire and realism give way to false sublimity. And the disposition should have pleased him greatly.

I

Attention to the basic device of exposition will help us; Act I, scene i establishes a theme for the play by pointing clearly to our question. Here, at his moment of self-declaration, Antony claims tragic status for love amidst the ruins of empire:

Danby's original essay by L. C. Knights in *Scrutiny*, XVI (1949), 318–23. These views, together with mine, supplement one another without duplication of method or approach.

> Let Rome in Tiber melt, and the wide arch
> Of the rang'd empire fall! Here is my space.
> Kingdoms are clay; our dungy earth alike
> Feeds beast as man; the nobleness of life
> Is to do thus, when such a mutual pair
> And such a twain can do't, in which I bind,
> On pain of punishment, the world to weet
> We stand up peerless.

This "nobleness of life," which a falling Rome is called upon to see as peerless, is a notion which Cleopatra will later take very seriously. Here, however, she adds to the satire directed at Antony's claim to nobility by terming it an "excellent falsehood," and by declaring that she will seem the fool she is not—"Antony will be himself." The opening lines of the scene already have invoked "this dotage of our general's," and have pointed to his "captain's heart" which "is become the bellows and the fan/ To cool a gipsy's lust."

> Take but good note, and you shall see in him
> The triple pillar of the world transform'd
> Into a strumpet's fool. Behold and see.

And the wry note is consistent; the scene which begins with Philo on the general's dotage ends with Demetrius on his public relations:

> I am full sorry
> That he approves the common liar, who
> Thus speaks of him at Rome.

Scene ii now shifts the theme of dedicated sensuality to lesser though equally explicit characters. Iras and Charmian, open it on a note of bickering with the fortuneteller over their future as whores for the great, and they conclude with some soothsaying of their own which promises sexual misfortune for Alexas. Here Enobarbus establishes his role

of amused participant and one-man chorus by remarking
in a line which sums up the episode, "Mine, and most of
our fortunes tonight shall be—drunk to bed." The protagonists are at last given their entry. Antony, whose new
mood is heralded by Cleopatra ("On the sudden/ A Roman
thought hath struck him."), faces first a messenger who
bears stiff news of the Parthian wars, and then the man
from Sicyon who is to tell of Fulvia's death. In the course
of the play Antony will often exhibit self-knowledge and
his revelation of it will occasionally be spurious, self-conscious, or even gravely comic. In depicting the whole
Antony, however, Shakespeare continually, and always at
the apt moment, redeems him from solemnity. After his
questionable claim to tragic afflatus in the opening scenes,
Antony's behavior with the messenger and Enobarbus
promptly restores him. The scene is so central and so ex-
pertly rendered that extensive quotation is needed:

> *Enter another* MESSENGER *with a letter.*
> *Antony.*   What are you?
> *Messenger.* Fulvia thy wife is dead.
> *Antony.*   Where died she?
> *Messenger.* In Sicyon:
>   Her length of sickness, with what else more serious
>   Importeth thee to know, this bears.
>   *Gives a letter.*
> *Antony.*   Forbear me.
>   *Exit* MESSENGER.
>   There's a great spirit gone! Thus did I desire it.
>   What our contempt doth often hurl from us,
>   We wish it ours again; the present pleasure,
>   By revolution low'ring, does become
>   The opposite of itself. She's good, being gone;
>   The hand could pluck her back that shov'd her on. . . .

Re-enter ENOBARBUS.

How now! Enobarbus!

Enobarbus. What's your pleasure, sir?

Antony. I must with haste from hence.

Enobarbus. Why, then we kill all our women. We see how mortal an unkindness is to them; if they suffer our departure, death's the word.

Antony. I must be gone.

Enobarbus. Under a compelling occasion, let women die. It were pity to cast them away for nothing; though, between them and a great cause, they should be esteemed nothing. Cleopatra, catching but the least noise of this, dies instantly; I have seen her die twenty times upon far poorer moment. I do think there is mettle in Death, which commits some loving act upon her, she hath such a celerity in dying. . . .

Antony. Would I had never seen her!

Enobarbus. O, sir, you had then left unseen a wonderful piece of work; which not to have been blest withal would have discredited your travel.

Antony. Fulvia is dead.

Enobarbus. Sir?

Antony. Fulvia is dead.

Enobarbus. Fulvia!

Antony. Dead.

Enobarbus. Why, sir, give the gods a thankful sacrifice. When it pleaseth their deities to take the wife of a man from him, it shows to man the tailors of the earth; comforting therein, that when old robes are worn out, there are members to make new. . . .

Antony. The business she hath broached in the state
Cannot endure my absence.

Enobarbus. And the business you have broach'd here cannot be without you; especially that of Cleopatra's, which wholly depends on your abode.

Antony. No more light answers. Let our officers
  Have notice what we purpose.

Contrast this scene with the one in which Brutus demon-
strates how a Stoic receives news of his wife's death. There
is a difference, naturally, between the Brutus-Portia and
Antony-Fulvia relationships, but it remains that Antony,
the half-maudlin epicure of scene i, who has wanted his
wife to die and now admits it with a sorrow which sur-
prises him, emerges with a dignity at least equal to that of
Brutus, the doctrinaire Stoic. The reason for this lies not
so much in Antony's code of honesty as in his manner, his
style, which will govern his really impressive moments
throughout the play. His stature will scarcely depend upon
his triumviral status, or his peerless grand passion, or his
repetitive and almost priggish self-examination in which
"Roman thoughts" abound. It will depend upon scenes like
the one just quoted which evoke respect for his worldly
intelligence, scenes in which his self-understanding is suggested but never intrusively expressed as it is in his more
solemn passages. This episode gives Antony an audience
advantage even over the winsome Enobarbus, who gets himself into trouble with oblivious babbling about "celerity in
dying" and escapes indignity solely through the forbearance, the unrebuking tact, of one who knows what indignity is. In evoking tragic response, the "woe or wonder"
in Shakespeare can become quite subordinate to effects of
this kind.

Was this understood, however, by Shakespeare's audience? The familiar voice of historical conscience cannot
be ignored. In answer to it, another and equally historical

voice may be heard: can we think of audience response in
Shakespeare's time as if it were adequately described by the
sparse records which have survived? We have no early accounts which specify *savoir-faire* in the hero as a major
element of tragedy, but this scarcely entitles us to say that
it was unmoving to Shakespeare's contemporaries, or that
its importance is eclipsed by the few specifications for
tragedy which they happened to set down and transmit to
us. Even at the risk of circular inference we must continue
to enlarge our conception of earlier playwriting from the
plays themselves. The limited contemporary comments
upon tragedy have their uses, but the commentary must be
balanced by internal evidence.

In a dramatic turn which sets him above previous satire,
Antony thus gains stature. The process is similar to Othello's
appearance after the scurrilous depiction of him by Iago
and Roderigo in their opening scene, with the exception,
of course, that Othello's conduct dramatically dispels an
untruth about him while Antony's qualifies an unfavorable
truth.

After allowing Antony his recovery, Shakespeare quickly
revives the satirical tone. When Roman gravity has tri-
umphed over Cleopatra's histrionics ("Cut my lace, Charmian, come!"), I.iv introduces Octavius who recasts Antony
in the earlier manner. He "is not more manlike/ Than
Cleopatra, nor the queen of Ptolemy/ More womanly than
he." It is now the turn of Lepidus, with his characteristic
heaviness, to announce the principle of tragic flaw:

>   I must not think there are
> Evils enow to darken all his goodness.
> His faults in him, seem as the spots of heaven,

More fiery by night's blackness; hereditary,
Rather than purchased; what he cannot change,
Than what he chooses.

This suggests Hamlet's "mole of nature," but with a senti-
mentality which Octavius promptly deflates:

You are too indulgent. Let's grant it is not
Amiss to tumble on the bed of Ptolemy;
To give a kingdom for a mirth; to sit
And keep the turn of tippling with a slave;
To reel the streets at noon, and stand the buffet
With knaves that smell of sweat: say this becomes him,—
As his composure must be rare indeed
Whom these things cannot blemish,—yet must Antony
No way excuse his foils, when we do bear
So great weight in his lightness. If he fill'd
His vacancy with his voluptuousness,
Full surfeits and the dryness of his bones
Call on him for't; but to confound such time
That drums him from his sport and speaks as loud
As his own state and ours, 'tis to be chid
As we rate boys who, being mature in knowledge,
Pawn their experience to their present pleasure,
And so rebel to judgement.

Octavius is thus given a choric function in which he questions Lepidus' bestowal upon Antony of the flawed hero's
role.

Scene v now ends the exposition in a mood of the earlier
soothsayer's scene. Its theme is again the sexually grotesque:
Cleopatra reflecting that the "unseminar'd" Mardian can
have no "freer thoughts" to stray forth from Egypt, as do
hers after the absent Antony; Cleopatra threatening, by
Isis, to give Charmian bloody teeth for presuming to compare Antony with Julius Caesar.

In the discussion of I.ii it was observed that Antony retains dignity in the face of satire not by virtue of his moral
conflict but because of his tact and worldly understanding.
The core of Act II enlarges this conception of Antony and
exhibits the same unpretentious quality in other characters;
their sharing of the trait points up Antony's possession of
it, just as the plain-dealing of Kent and the Fool augments
Cordelia's frankness in *Lear*. That Shakespeare considers
the urbane opportunism of Enobarbus, Pompey, Menas,
and Antony to lack ultimate wisdom may be assumed, but
he clearly wishes us to admire men who know what they
are and, without straining at it, play a role for what it is.

Enobarbus introduces the note in dialogue with Lepidus
at the opening of II.ii. The triumvirate is to meet and the
session is likely to be violent; Enobarbus observes that if
he were the wearer of Antony's beard today, he would
leave it unshaven for the challenge by plucking, and Lepidus, a kind of Polonius, counters with the sober line: " 'Tis
not a time for private stomaching." This follows:

> *Enobarbus.*   Every time
>   Serves for the matter that is then born in't.
> *Lepidus*. But small to greater matters must give way.
> *Enobarbus*. Not if the small come first.

Enter the adversaries and both prophets are proved wrong,
for matters equally great and small are discussed with the
scene ending in conciliation. Antony gains his stature
through contrast with Octavius: Caesar's heir starts with
a perfect advantage, for Antony's situation is close to the
Prodigal Son's, but Octavius quickly loses face and is finally
led to increasing petulance as Antony's self-possession
needles him:

Caesar. You have broken
  The article of your oath; which you shall never
  Have tongue to charge me with.
Lepidus. Soft, Caesar!
Antony. No,
  Lepidus, let him speak.
  The honour is sacred which he talks on now,
  Supposing that I lack'd it. But, on, Caesar:
  The article of my oath.
Caesar. To lend me arms and aid when I requir'd them;
  The which you both denied.
Antony. Neglected, rather;
  And then when poisoned hours had bound me up
  From mine own knowledge. As nearly as I may,
  I'll play the penitent to you; but mine honesty
  Shall not make poor my greatness, nor my power
  Work without it. Truth is, that Fulvia,
  To have me out of Egypt, made wars here;
  For which myself, the ignorant motive, do
  So far ask pardon as befits mine honour
  To stoop in such a case.
Lepidus. 'Tis noble spoken

"But, on, Caesar." The old sybarite who could keep the
turn of tippling with a slave can quietly rise both to the
occasion and to a plane of dignity.

  This is the Antony of consequence. As usual, however,
the other Antony quickly offsets him. The celebrated lines
on Cleopatra's barge can be quoted both by those who
admire and those who condemn Shakespeare's mixing of
sublimity with egoistic sensuality. It would seem, however,
that the admirers and the detractors are equally wrong here,
for the sublimity of the passage is modified by deliberate
anticlimax. As Enobarbus completes for the wide-eyed
Agrippa his account of Cleopatra descending the Nile

amidst lovesick winds and the stroke of silver oars timed
to the music of flutes, the camera-like focus moves to the
shore, upon which is seen Antony:

> *Enobarbus*. . . . and Antony
>   Enthron'd in' th' market-place, did sit alone,
>   Whistling to th' air, which, but for vacancy,
>   Had gone to gaze on Cleopatra too
>   And made a gap in nature.
> *Agrippa*.   Rare Egyptian!
> *Enobarbus*. Upon her landing, Antony sent to her,
>   Invited her to supper. She replied,
>   It should be better he became her guest;
>   Which she entreated. Our courteous Antony,
>   Whom ne'er the word of "No" woman heard speak,
>   Being barber'd ten times o'er, goes to the feast,
>   And for his ordinary pays his heart
>   For what his eyes eat only.

Closely following this passage is another grotesque scene
(II.v), hovered over as before by Mardian the eunuch, who
will play with Cleopatra (at billiards) "as well as I can,
Madam." Here the audience hears Cleopatra's story of
Antony and the salted fish, and is treated to her scene with
the messenger. After she "hales him up and down" she
orders him whipped with wire and washed with brine, all
for bringing her news of Antony and Octavia. "Is he married?"—"He's married"—"He is married?"—"He is married?"—"He's married to Octavia." So runs the refrain ending an episode which is at once magnificent and prepos-
terous.

In the two scenes which follow (the council with Pompey
and the feast aboard his galley) a group of characters is
used to reintroduce the note of ironical competence and

poise which has so effectively graced Antony. Pompey has
Hotspur's astringent traits with little of the urge to pluck
bright honor from the pale-faced moon; Enobarbus is himself. Lepidus, the bibulous second-rater, is a foil; inadequate
in his cups as in his political life, he becomes a butt almost
literally in the manner of Polonius as Antony tells him of
the crocodile which is shaped like itself, is as broad as itself,
and moves "with its own organs." "Very like a crocodile,"
Polonius would have answered. When it is remarked of
the servant who carries Lepidus out that a strong back is
needed to lift the world's third part, there are suggestions
that the burden is not heavy. For unlike the others Lepidus
is subdued to what he works in; when he treads in moral
"quick-sands" (Antony's term), he merely flounders.

An exchange between Pompey and Menas, however, suggests most clearly the ethical void in which Antony flourishes. These two are characters who attain dignity, and by
analogy reflect it upon Antony, not because they set themselves above morality, but because they do so easily and
with no effort to be impressive. Withdraw this saving grace
from the nonconformist and simple egotism remains. It is
a grace, incidentally, which marks Shaw's own Andrew
Undershaft who would have been comfortable with Pompey and Menas.

> *Menas.* Wilt thou be lord of all the world?
> *Pompey.*   What say'st thou?
> *Menas.* Wilt thou be lord of the whole world? That's twice.
> *Pompey.* How should that be?
> *Menas.*   But entertain it,
>   And, though thou think me poor, I am the man
>   Will give thee all the world.
> *Pompey.*   Hast thou drunk well?

Menas. No, Pompey, I have kept me from the cup.
   Thou art, if thou dar'st be, the earthly Jove.
   Whate'er the ocean pales, or sky inclips,
   Is thine, if thou wilt ha't.
Pompey.   Show me which way.
Menas. These three world-sharers, these competitors,
   Are in thy vessel: let me cut the cable;
   And, when we are put off, fall to their throats.
   All there is thine.
Pompey.   Ah, this thou shouldst have done,
   And not have spoke on't! In me 'tis villany;
   In thee 't had been good service. Thou must know,
   'Tis not my profit that does lead mine honour;
   Mine honour, it. Repent that e'er thy tongue
   Hath so betray'd thine act. Being done unknown,
   I should have found it afterwards well done,
   But must condemn it now. Desist, and drink.
Menas. [*Aside*] For this,
   I'll never follow thy pall'd fortunes more.

Here is the Antony-Enobarbus relationship in miniature, save that Menas is untroubled by Enobarbus' engaging sense of the absurd. But the parallel is more than one of substance; again the redeeming quality lies in manner and word which show the quality beneath: "Wilt thou be lord of the whole world? That's twice."

By the end of Act II the satirical and affirmative elements of the play are present in excellent proportion. At this point also, the fortunes of Antony rest in balance. Act III abruptly brings the descent, and in keeping with the satirical and realistic tone previously set, the fall is not "dramatic" like that of Macbeth or Othello; Antony, who has ridden high in *Realpolitik* ending in marriage with Octavia of the "holy, cold, and still conversation," simply and surely reverts. In scene vi, reports from Alexandria declare that "Cleopatra and himself," surrounded by Caesarion "and all the unlawful issue that their lust/ . . . hath made between them," have been publicly enthroned. "As 'tis reported, so," says Caesar, and Maecenas adds, in one of those beautifully understated lines, "Let Rome be thus inform'd." Conventional "catastrophe" is at a minimum. In scene vii, after Enobarbus has told Cleopatra that Antony has been "traduc'd for levity" and that Romans believe "Photinus an eunuch and your maids/ Manage this war," the decision of Antony to fight by sea is set down as imbecile by three choric characters in workman-like succession: Enobarbus, Canidius, and the significant common soldier. In scene x, only twenty lines later, comes a report of the naval battle. It is a sight that has "blasted" Enobarbus' eyes; he and Scarus describe it in Shakespeare's full range of satirical eloquence which even lampoons Antony's role as "noble ruin."

Scarus.   Yon ribaldried nag of Egypt,—
  Whom leprosy o'ertake!—i' th' midst o' th' fight,
  When vantage like a pair of twins appear'd,
  Both as the same, or rather ours the elder,
  The breeze upon her, like a cow in June,
  Hoists sails and flies.
Enobarbus. That I beheld.
  Mine eyes did sicken at the sight and could not
  Endure a further view.
Scarus.   She once being loof'd,
  The noble ruin of her magic, Antony,
  Claps on his sea-wing, and, like a doting mallard,
  Leaving the fight in height, flies after her.
  I never saw an action of such shame;
  Experience, manhood, honor, ne'er before
  Did violate so itself.

A few lines later, in scene xi, Antony declares that he has
fled himself and has instructed cowards how to run; pathetically he offers his friends treasure and passage if they will
only leave him. In subsequent dialogue he charges Cleopatra
with leading him to dishonor, and receives from her the immortal reply,

> O my lord, my lord,
> Forgive my fearful sails! I little thought
> You would have followed.

But immediately he is willing to be rewarded for disaster
with a caress: "Even this repays me." Soon after, Enobarbus
when asked by Cleopatra, "What shall we do?" replies,
"Think and die."

Antony now offers his plan for personal combat with
Caesar, which is capped by Enobarbus' line, "Caesar, thou
hast subdu'd/ His judgement too." In scene xiii, Shakespeare
skillfully ends the lugubrious crisis with an episode parallel
to II.v in which Cleopatra ordered the messenger to be
whipped. Here another messenger, Thyreus, is discovered
by Antony as he takes Cleopatra by the hand, and by the
time he is flogged is doubtless in agreement with Enobarbus—" 'Tis better playing with a lion's whelp/ Than with
an old one dying." The lapse from *noblesse oblige* is presented as noisy domestic strife, screaming at the servants;
in order to keep Antony's fall within the set limits of realism and satire, Shakespeare has him vent his shame upon the
first available scapegoat, and reinforces realism of motive
with realism of action by stressing the grotesque, verbally
repetitive cruelty of such a situation. "Take hence this Jack
and whip him/ . . . Whip him! . . ./ Till like a boy, you
see him cringe his face./ . . . Take him hence./ . . . Tug

him away. Being whipp'd,/ Bring him again; this Jack of
Caesar shall/ Bear us an errand to him." And afterward:

Antony. Is he whipp'd?
Servant. Soundly, my lord.
Antony. Cried he? and begg'd a pardon?
Servant. He did ask favour.
Antony. [*to the messenger*] If that thy father live, let him
    repent
  Thou wast not made his daughter; and be thou sorry
  To follow Caesar in his triumph, since
  Thou hast been whipp'd for following him.

In the interval between the order for whipping and its execution Antony has addressed Cleopatra as a "boggler ever"
whom he found "as a morsel cold upon/ Dead Caesar's
trencher." "O, that I were/ Upon the hill of Basan, to out-
roar/ The horned herd!" As the scene ends, however, the
old infatuation returns, for the catharsis of the whipped
Jack enables Antony to call for yet another "gaudy night"
in which he and the "sad captains" will "mock the midnight
bell," and "the wine peep through their scars."

It is a deceptive quality in Shakespeare that scenes of
down-at-the-heels passion are often rendered with rhetorical magnificence. Witness Lear's, Goneril's, and Regan's
curses bestowed upon one another in the "domestic" episodes, or Othello's superb lines in the scene he contrives
with Desdemona as whore and Emilia as procuress. Splendid
rhetoric may cause the unwary to think that the rage it
expresses is splendid, and of course in a very limited sense
it is. In the scene of Antony's wild anger and reconciliation,
however, it appears that Shakespeare wished to forestall
such interpretation with direct comment. After the Jack
is whipped and the lovers have made up, Enobarbus, who is

hardly one of Shaw's Puritans, ends the matter quietly and
pointedly:

>   I see still
> A diminution in our captain's brain
> Restores his heart.

As Enobarbus thus ruefully concludes Act III, the de-
grading of Antony is intensified in IV.i by Octavius:

> He calls me boy, and chides as he had power
> To beat me out of Egypt. My messenger
> He hath whipp'd with rods; dares me to personal combat,
> Caesar to Antony. Let the old ruffian know
> I have many other ways to die; meantime
> Laugh at his challenge.

And the diminution in our captain's brain is finally confirmed with Antony's puzzlement over news brought by
Domitius that Octavius rejects the absurd challenge.

In a brief but affecting scene, Antony now calls upon
his followers to tend him, to scant not his cups, an action
which reduces them to tears and evokes comment from
Enobarbus which again qualifies sympathy with clear insight: "Look they weep;/ And I, an ass, am onion eyed."
There follows the premonitory music "i' th' air" and "under
the earth," a sign, the soldiers say, that the god Hercules
whom Antony loved "now leaves him." Casual, inexorable
collapse; scene v brings the abandonment of Antony by
Enobarbus, and the succeeding one briefly shows Enobarbus, stricken by Antony's generosity, seeking out "some
ditch wherein to die."

The rhythm of triumph and defeat has begun to quicken:
within less than a hundred lines (scenes viii to xii. 15) the
narrative takes Antony from sinister victory ("O infinite

virtue, com'st thou smiling from/ The world's great snare
uncaught?") to the depth of betrayal, at which he names
Cleopatra as the "triple turn'd whore" who has "sold"
him "to this novice." I have tried to describe Act IV in the
terse manner of its action in order to suggest that plot structure itself expresses Antony's descent. At the close of Act
III he enters a limbo of quick movement toward ruin in
which his defiance and submission become increasingly
automatic. It is true that this quality of both the character
and the action is often explained by imagining a tired or
hurried Shakespeare who from Act III onward began to
write short scenes and to follow Plutarch's narrative order.
The weariness or hurry is anyone's guess. The increased
tempo and flattened tone of the descent, however, are perfectly in keeping with tragedy in which the hero is not
struck down but is progressively diminished; Enobarbus'
use of the word "diminution" may be supposed to approxi-
mate the truth.

As Shakespeare's weariness fails to account adequately for
the fifteen laconic scenes of Act IV, so does the curtainless
Elizabethan stage—the chain of scenes would be unsatis-
factory on any stage if it violated a rhythm previously
established in the tragedy. Far from breaking such a rhythm,
the accelerated sequence fulfills it. The play begins with
a slow alternation between grandeur and ignominy, and as
it advances this tempo increases until the end of Act IV.
There, appropriately, it slows and stops.

At this point Shakespeare returns to the note heard in
the opening exposition, the theme of high tragedy itself
which came close to parody in Antony's vision of the
"nobleness of life." In Act I this vision was mocked or re-

jected by several characters, including Cleopatra, but it is now her turn to claim the amenities of tragedy as the full play of satire is resumed. Antony, however, will no longer strain at sublimity and will grow in stature because of his reticence.

Act IV, scene xv arises from the decision of Cleopatra, advised by Charmian in scene xiii, to repossess Antony by withdrawing and sending word that she is dead. "To th' monument!/ Mardian, go tell him I have slain myself." And with a child's casual effrontery: "Hence, Mardian,/ And bring me how he takes my death." The monument scene with its frequently sentimentalized lines ("I am dying, Egypt, dying . . .") thus stems directly from a desire of Cleopatra to create situation, to write her own tragedy.[3]

As he is brought to his end by the false news of Cleopatra's death, Antony's last words express no spurious sublimity. He seems almost to anticipate Shaw's "wretched end of the business" by speaking of his fate as a "miserable change" which his followers must neither "lament nor sorrow at." True, he recalls his role as "the noblest," but here he describes his former status which he plainly distinguishes from the miserable change. He asks only to die "not basely," not "cowardly [to] put off my helmet to/ My countryman." Cleopatra, however, does assert the grand descent, and a familiar egoism colors her statement:

> Noblest of men, woo 't die?
> Hast thou no care of me? Shall I abide
> In this dull world, which in thy absence is
> No better than a sty? O, see, my women.
> The crown o' th' earth doth melt. My lord!

[3] Her "practical" motive, to win back Antony, is in no way exclusive of this one.

O, wither'd is the garland of the war,
The soldier's pole is fall'n! Young boys and girls
Are level now with men; the odds is gone,
And there is nothing left remarkable
Beneath the visiting moon.

To say that the sentiment of this passage is merely selfish would be as untrue as to say that it amounts to genuine renunciation. Perhaps, as some have believed, we do have a new Cleopatra here, but in a contextual reading of these lines there must still be heard the old one who created the scene, not too unwittingly, for herself. She has become the chorus of conventional tragedy even to the extent of rendering inversely the doctrine of "admiration" or wonder ("there is nothing left remarkable/ Beneath the visiting moon"). And after invoking Antony as the "noblest of men" she bestows the same nobility upon her coterie:

My noble girls! . . .
Our lamp is spent, it's out!

The "girls" are thus endowed by Cleopatra with the stuff of tragedy; had Mardian been on hand there is the off-chance that he might have been translated too.

If this interpretation suggests an irony too modern, the possible anachronism may be tested by referring to V.i and V.ii. Again Shakespeare follows the plan of his early exposition by allowing orthodox notions of fallen grandeur to be stated and then questioned.[4] Act V, scene i presents a galaxy of stock comment upon tragic stature and tragic flaw; it is very nearly a manual of the subject, and it is hard to understand why it has not been emphasized in discussions of Elizabethan critical doctrine. As Dercetas acquaints

---

[4] Questioned not in substance but in application.

Octavius, Maecenas, and others with news of Antony's
death, dialogue ensues in which each speaker amplifies the
convention. First, from Octavius, there is the concept of
magnitude, of world-wide convulsion.

> The breaking of so great a thing should make
> A greater crack. The round world
> Should have shook lions into civil streets,
> And citizens to their dens. The death of Antony
> Is not a single doom; in the name lay
> A moiety of the world.

Now Agrippa, who seems to be thinking of fate, flaw, and
compulsion: "strange it is/ That nature must compel us to
lament/ Our most persisted deeds." And Maecenas specifically on the flaw principle: "His taints and honours/ Wag'd
equal with him." Next, Agrippa must show that he understands this:

> A rarer spirit never
> Did steer humanity; but you gods will give us
> Some faults to make us men.

Then appears the *de casibus* theory with the mirror for
magistrates. As Agrippa declares that "Caesar is touched,"
Maecenas explains: "When such a spacious mirror's set before him,/ He needs must see himself." Finally Octavius
again, with a summation:

> O Antony!
> I have followed thee to this; but we do lance
> Diseases in our bodies. I must perforce
> Have shown to thee such a declining day,
> Or look on thine; we could not stall together
> In the whole world: but yet let me lament,
> With tears as sovereign as the blood of hearts,
> That thou, my brother, my competitor

In top of all design, my mate in empire,
Friend and companion in the front of war,
The arm of mine own body, and the heart
Where mine his thoughts did kindle,—that our stars,
Unreconcilable, should divide
Our equalness to this. Hear me, good friends,—
But I will tell you at some meeter season.

Dolabella, however, is elsewhere and if we read the next
scene in context we may intuit the reason. After the retinue
of Octavius has been converted to a chorus and has presented the subject of tragedy in every standard detail,
Cleopatra promptly continues the theme [5] in scene ii with
a vision of Antony's stature and flaw. Dolabella, however,
is apparently assigned the function of reducing her illusion
in a single, well-turned line. As he confronts Cleopatra she
loses no time in leading to the issue.

Cleopatra. I dream'd there was an Emperor Antony.
  O, such another sleep, that I might see
  But such another man!
Dolabella.   If it might please ye,—
Cleopatra. His face was as the heavens; and therein stuck
  A sun and moon, which kept their course and lighted
  The little O, the earth.
Dolabella.   Most sovereign creature,—
Cleopatra. His legs bestrid the ocean; his rear'd arm

---

[5] That the conception of tragic nobility is being carried over as a theme
from V.i to V.ii is apparent from a passage (V.ii.41–46) which occurs
between the two passages under consideration.

  Cleopatra.   What of death too,
    That rids our dogs of languish?
  Proculeius.   Cleopatra,
    Do not abuse my master's bounty by
    Th' undoing of yourself. Let the world see
    His nobleness well acted, which your death
    Will never let come forth.

> Crested the world; his voice was propertied
> As all the tuned spheres. . . .
>   His delights
> Were dolphin-like: they show'd his back above
> The element they liv'd in. In his livery
> Walk'd crowns and crownets; realms and islands were
> As plates dropp'd from his pocket.
> *Dolabella.*   Cleopatra!

Note Dolabella's interruptions which seem to imply that a public airing of nobility in these terms approaches travesty and destroys a dignity which should be maintained by reticence. Note that the climax of Cleopatra's fantasy dwells upon Antony's sensuality, his "delights." Like the dolphin they rise with Antony above their element in a perfect image of the tragic protagonist who transcends his world of evil. Note finally how the fantasy is rejected. Turning to Dolabella just after her lines on Antony and the dolphin, Cleopatra puts the ultimate question: "Think you there was or might be such a man/ As this I dream'd of?" And Dolabella in one line of memorable timing: "Gentle madam, no." Here is one of the shortest dramatic commentaries on record, and its choric nature is warranted. Plot development, narration, calls merely for Dolabella to inform Cleopatra of Caesar's intention to lead her through Rome in triumph. Shakespeare, however, expands the situation into dialogue between a romanticist and a sympathetic realist on the subject of Antony's role as tragic hero.

We should not interpret V.i–V.ii as a simplified denial of tragic dignity. Even Dolabella, after rejecting Cleopatra's vision, qualifies himself: "Your loss is as yourself, great." And the previous "colloquium" on tragedy is modified,[6] not rejected, by Cleopatra's excesses on the theme it introduced. Of one thing, however, we can be sure; Cleopatra colors the issue with her notions of the sublime, and Dolabella anticipates Shaw in denying the scale of grandeur she finds in her dolphin-protagonist. In Shaw's words, but with a contrary application, realism is allowed to "have its demonstration," and at a key point of the tragedy.

The end is well known—Cleopatra and the asp, with lines such as "Finish good lady; the bright day is done,/ And we are for the dark." It would be foolish and unnecessary to say that Cleopatra's descent is unmoving. But it is unperceptive to see it as the august event she desires. As it runs its final course she is caught concealing a large portion of her goods and money in a statement to Caesar which Seleucus, her treasurer, refuses to verify. Her response is to berate Seleucus in an ignominious scene which is ended by still another assertion of her royal claim to tragedy. This time her pose is unmistakably tinged with the comic for she ascribes all elements of pettiness in her "fall" to Seleucus who, after all, simply told the truth when she called upon him, characteristically, for a dramatic fib. With Seleucus shouldering the pettiness, Cleopatra's inimitable logic can now claim the dignity:

[6] If it is objected that the interesting presentation in V.i of the stock notions of tragedy is an entirely serious one, and that the dialogue of the scene formally confers upon Antony the standard traits of a tragic hero, I can only repeat that in V.ii Cleopatra restates the essence of V.i in her "dolphin" vision, which is qualified, as described, by Dolabella. Act V, scene i and V.ii should thus be considered together as an elaborate consideration of the tragic role (this would include the passage mentioned in footnote 5, p. 179); and it should be observed that V.ii, not V.i, provides, dramatically speaking, the qualifying note. Each passage should be read in the context of the other.

> Be it known that we, the greatest, are misthought
> For things that others do; and, when we fall,
> We answer others' merits [Seleucus's demerits] in our
>   name,
> Are therefore to pitied.

Pity for the "fall" of "the greatest"—the traditional vocabulary of tragedy—and Cleopatra uses it to put a solemn face on matters which are far from solemn. In Plutarch's version of the Seleucus incident, Octavius "fell a laughing." Here Octavius may be more decorous, but Shakespeare's major change in the scene points to an ironical purpose. In Plutarch, Seleucus, unasked, eagerly exposes Cleopatra in order to please Caesar; [7] in Shakespeare, Cleopatra calls Seleucus forth, ordering him to corroborate her story, and it is only then that he tells the truth, asserting "peril" to be his motive. Cleopatra's line, "the greatest are misthought/ For things that others do," could thus be a moving one in the situation given by Plutarch. In the one Shakespeare provides, her extraction of tragedy from the incident is something less, or more, than moving.

Thus in *Antony and Cleopatra* the quality of tragedy, as an attribute of the protagonists, is an actual issue within the tragedy itself. It is a theme which appears in the exposition and is resumed with great particularity toward the close of the play. When the protagonists self-consciously assume a flawed stature, the role is ironically denied them; when they are simply themselves they achieve a subdued dignity. The dignity, however, is qualified by satire which constantly keeps the tragedy within bounds of moral realism.

At the play's end, however, do Caesar's words pro-

---

[7] *Shakespeare's Plutarch*, ed. Tucker Brooke, II, 130.

nounced over the "pair so famous" deny the satire and
introduce what Shaw called "theatrical sublimity?"

> Take up her bed;
> And bear her women from the monument.
> She shall be buried by her Antony;
> No grave upon the earth shall clip in it
> A pair so famous. High events as these
> Strike those that make them; and their story is
> No less in pity than his glory which
> Brought them to be lamented. Our army shall
> In solemn show attend this funeral;
> And then to Rome. Come, Dolabella, see
> High order in this great solemnity.

The travesty of fallen grandeur in Cleopatra's encounter
with Seleucus immediately precedes the episode which these
lines conclude. And it is interesting that Octavius bestows
upon Cleopatra the same tragic dignity she had assumed for
herself in the Seleucus scene. There she had laid dubious
claim to pity for the fall of "the greatest," and here Caesar
grants her fame, and a pity equal to his own glory. In short,
a subject of comedy (see Plutarch) has within two hundred
lines become a theme of high seriousness which ends the
play.

In most tragedies this would be a reversal of tone and
point of view. Had Brutus been given lines toward the end
of *Julius Caesar* in which he had described himself, amidst
laughter from the audience, as the noblest Roman of them
all, the speech of Antony which concludes the play on that
note would have suffered, and not mildly. The tragedy, in
fact, would have been maimed at the point of Brutus' statement. In *Antony and Cleopatra*, however, just this kind of
a situation is successful, and for the obvious reason that

Antony and Cleopatra is not at all like *Julius Caesar*. The latter play is "straight" tragedy, the former a tragedy in which satire and seriousness are in continual suspension. The satire, moreover, is directed constantly at claims of tragic stature which the protagonists assert for themselves. Consistently then, the suspension of opposites is carried through to the end: in the Seleucus incident Cleopatra's claim, for herself, of the *de casibus* role is comic; in Caesar's lines her posthumous assumption of the role is not at all comic.

If we are asked which of these concluding notes should prevail, the answer, I believe, is that neither is controlling. Each supplies context for the other and the balanced result agrees perfectly with a tone set throughout; anything other than this blend of satire and tragedy would have destroyed a quality present from the beginning. Caesar's lines ask us, of course, to respect death and the dead, and there is no mockery in them. But if context has meaning, Shakespeare is not asking us to forego smiles when we remember Seleucus.

II

Although *Antony and Cleopatra* may contain its own answer to moralists in the Shaw tradition, it is possible that their objection is met at considerable cost. If, in denying a shift from satire to false sublimity, we find that the play is dominantly ironical—that it qualifies conventional nobility even in the "fall"—and if we limit Antony to occasional virtues of frankness and poise, have we not cut both the play and its characters down to size? Do we not end with drama which is excellent realism but doubtful tragedy?

The problem is complicated by Antony's clear but somewhat spurious grasp of his own limitations. His self-perception is complete but it is often brashly indulgent. In the character of Othello there is a core of self-knowledge which dramatically replaces delusion at the end, and which, unlike Antony's self-awareness, appears cleanly in a single crisis. Othello's insight into his error is neither chronic nor sentimental. Macbeth's commitment to evil in the face of clear moral understanding is similar to Antony's, and his expression of self-knowledge is also repetitive. Yet there is a great difference: Macbeth's obsession is one induced and maintained by supernatural evil which controls him after his surrender to the instruments of darkness; his recurrent conscience is in conflict with forces which are both formidable and intangible. On the other hand, Antony's obsession is entirely carnal, entirely of this world; while clearly understandable it is convincing because it is a human weakness, not a demonic urge. And by dwelling almost fondly upon it, Antony scarcely makes it a mature frailty.

Lear's pride is as marked as Antony's sensuality, but his regeneration, of course, is the essence of the play. Antony, however, never really changes, for he knows himself from the beginning as he drifts to what Shaw called the wretched end of the business. Hamlet's self-knowledge is on the grand scale of sensing that he can never know himself. His character is so intricate that his appraisal of it often appears arbitrary or incomplete. The delusion of Brutus, if his motives amount to actual delusion, is both tacit and complex, and his flaw is so plainly related to excess virtue that

the crack-in-the-splendid-armor doctrine of tragedy fits
him perfectly; no character in Shakespeare contrasts more
relevantly and completely with Antony.

On the basis of Hamlet's "mole of nature" speech and of
the lines spoken by Agrippa, Maecenas, and Cleopatra (see
pp. 177–80), there is no doubt that Shakespeare understood the role in tragedy of the flawed hero.[8] Nor is there
doubt that he accepted a relationship between social rank
and tragic stature. But when the highly placed hero becomes the military sensualist who loses battles in a ludicrous
manner, when his self-perceived imperfection becomes a
doting satyriasis, the quality of transcended flaw becomes
uncertain. It becomes doubly uncertain after Cleopatra
likens Antony's sensuality to the dolphin rising above its
element, only to have Dolabella question the comparison.
The spectacle of Antony may be both colorful and pitiful
but it is not the spectacle of a shamed yet laconic Othello,
or of a Macbeth whose function is smothered in surmise.

The problem we have been framing is not confined in
Shakespeare to *Antony and Cleopatra*. Only occasionally
has this play been questioned on the ground that its protagonists lack stature; others, however—*Timon of Athens*
and *Coriolanus*, to say nothing of *Titus Andronicus* which
we will not consider—have consistently been placed in a
lesser rank of tragedy. We are not concerned at the moment
with the inferiority of these plays as dramatic and poetic

---

[8] By his understanding of the principle I do not mean his acceptance
of it in the play at hand. As for Hamlet's "mole of nature" lines, it is true
that they are not literally a statement of the tragic flaw conception, but
the various assertions of this fact fail to demonstrate that the passage does
not strongly suggest the idea. It requires confidence to say that an
Elizabethan spectator would not get the implication as well as the literal
meaning.

art; we are interested in the conventional opinion that they are second-rate tragedies because their title characters are second rate. It would be hard to deny, of course, that Timon and Coriolanus are destroyed by narrow crotchets, or that they sadly lack redeeming insight or self-understanding. Such appraisals are obviously true ones because they are based upon the very point made in both plays; in each the tragedy has been written around a hero deliberately conceived as not-Hamlet, not-Lear, or not-Othello. Timon tries to achieve magnificence but can only exhibit Veblen's "conspicuous waste." Frustrated in the noblesse he aims for, he asserts its pseudo-opposite, a Thersitean misanthropy and scurrility. Coriolanus is even less complex; he loves war and detests plebeians at the beginning and he does so at the end.[9] Both protagonists are rigid and can only be destroyed by egoism whereas Lear and Othello are destroyed in transcending it.

There is also *Romeo and Juliet* to consider. Conspicuous among the platitudes of Shakespeare study is the description of this play as a tragedy not of character but of circumstance. Although the implications are sometimes puzzling, the intent of such a statement is clear: Romeo and Juliet, because they are immature, lack the understanding or power to be responsible for their own destruction. There is little in the idea with which to quarrel except the suggestion it carries that the play lacks stature. Like *Timon* and *Coriolanus*, *Romeo and Juliet* is supposed to be a lesser tragedy because its protagonists are lesser characters.

[9] His sudden submission to Volumnia's plea for Rome (V.iii.182–93) is far more of a capitulation to his mother because she is his mother than it is a victory of insight. See Volumnia's words (lines 153–182) as well as Menenius' comments (V.iv.55–60), and compare Coriolanus' "conversion" with Othello's or Lear's.

These plays, then, require an extension of the original issue. We began by asking whether *Antony and Cleopatra* could limit and satirize tragic noblesse and yet remain a tragedy; after considering *Romeo and Juliet, Timon,* and *Coriolanus,* we find that the problem in Shakespeare of a deliberately minimized hero is both extensive and varied.

Some historians could settle this problem by stressing the turn of Fortune's wheel and the awesomeness of death as defining norms of Elizabethan tragedy. For them the issue would not exist because all four of the plays mentioned contain these elements, and the absence of stature-in-insight would be of little significance. As usual, however, such a judgment requires us to assume that surviving Elizabethan definitions are not reductive, that lack of complexity in definition means a lack of complexity in the thing defined. Such an assumption produces incomplete history, and we may doubt that it would have satisfied Shakespeare who seems to have been more experimental than most of his contemporaries. In any event, the supposedly historical standards fail to encompass our own experience with the plays.

Another response to our question would be to disown it as an invasion of art by morals—to ask what difference it makes whether Antony is a weary but knowing sensualist or Timon a crabbed misanthrope. Life is like that, some believe, and Shakespeare never ran away from it. True, but this evades the problem. Mere suspension of moral judgment will not induce or account for the tragic response, for when we abstain from judgment of the hero we in no way imply, necessarily, that he has asserted value or dignity in his fall.

More discriminating amoralists will offer a different objection. The whole question of tragic effect, they will say, is unrelated to ethical ideas which have been employed mistakenly in judgment of the protagonist, and thus of the play in which he appears. Although the given tragedy may imply a moral universe and although the hero may gain stature within it, tragedy is finally a quality which stems from art, not from religiosity or ethical insight. Certain critics, for example, believe that patterns or rhythms of life expressed in the structure and detail of a tragedy account for the value we place upon it. There are a number of such views in which stature-in-defeat, an ethical factor, is looked upon as nonintrinsic. I can only say, however, that I find it intrinsic and cannot see how the various nonmoral views of tragedy replace it or, for that matter, are at all incompatible with it. Argument on this assumption would be confusing here; we shall have to agree that only those who share it will be concerned with the discussion which follows.

Granted that dignity—maturity of insight and action displaying it—is a necessary element of tragedy, what happens when the tragic hero fails in some way to possess it? If certain of Shakespeare's protagonists are said to lack it, is there an implied failure, as tragedy, of the plays in which they appear?

Perhaps this question can be answered in terms provided by Shakespeare himself. In five tragedies, *Julius Caesar, Hamlet, Lear, Othello,* and *Macbeth,* he presented heroes who achieve a rare level of perception which is neither self-indulgent nor indecisive. In one, *Romeo and Juliet,* he gave us characters who are immature to the point of "star-cross'd" innocence. In two, *Timon* and *Coriolanus,* he

drastically limited the insight of the central figure. Finally,
in *Antony and Cleopatra* he offered protagonists who combine impressive qualities with an artless and self-conscious
claim to the "nobleness of life," which is satirized almost
to the end. More, he used some of the traditional concepts
of tragedy ironically as themes for choric dialogue. It is
apparent that Shakespeare "diminished" his hero in at least
a third of the tragedies he wrote.

Does this suggest a factor other than the hero as mainly
responsible for the tragic effect? I believe that it may; I suggest that Shakespeare saw tragic insight as a quality of the
play, and only secondarily, although often, as a quality of
the protagonist. This would mean, for example, that the
perception of tragic "predicament," of man's fate, was the
function not primarily of Hamlet but of *Hamlet*. It happens in this case that the character himself contributes
extensively to the tragic response, but Shakespeare may
not have considered this as essential. If we turn again to
Coriolanus we may see the problem in a form which is both
historical and universal. The play itself advances a crisis
vivid to Shakespeare's age, the clash of privilege and authority with popular discontent. In the nature of things,
such a crisis often ends in stalemate: those who have learned
nothing of the present, and have forgotten nothing of the
past, collide in futility with those who foreshadow the
future but cannot cope with the present. Shakespeare could
have given Coriolanus some of the traits of Menenius, but
instead he set a stiff protagonist against a wavering populace, with the discerning Menenius caught between un-
reasoning opposites. And from the play, certainly not from
the insight of its hero, comes significant truth in the spec-

tacle of a society dying. The dignity of perception underlying a Shakespearian tragedy, and communicated with
art to an audience either Elizabethan or modern, is its essential quality. But in his own right the protagonist may
share the perception or he may not.

This would suggest that a "satirical tragedy" [10] like *Antony and Cleopatra* is in no sense anomalous. Although spirited it is soberly honest; although astringent it is sympathetic; and although realistic in outlook it contains great art.
It has the stature, whether or not the hero attains greatness,
and it, not Antony or Cleopatra, embodies the ultimate
insight intended for an audience. *Antony and Cleopatra*
asserts human dignity, value, because it confronts defeat
with a superb expression of ironical truth. As the audience
joins in the confrontation and expression, it perceives events
not in the manner of Antony or Cleopatra but of Shakespeare.

It is interesting that present-day tragedy can be justified
in similar fashion. We hear repeatedly that our age has
lost the tragic sense because we restrict ourselves to characters like Oswald in *Ghosts*, Clyde Griffiths in *An American Tragedy*, or Willy Loman in *The Death of a Salesman*.
It may be that these efforts fail as tragedies, but if so it
is not because their central characters admittedly lack stature or comprehension. Again, the dignity and insight may
lie in the work of art which contains the character, and
this may account for the reader who is moved deeply but
feels he should not be, since critics have told him either

---

[10] This term is different in meaning from O. J. Campbell's "tragical
satire" (*Shakespeare's Satires*, Oxford, 1943). It is not, however, a denial
of his conception; Mr. Campbell does not include *Antony and Cleopatra*
in his study.

that tragedy is dead [11] or that it awaits resurrection through rebirth of the discerning hero. Such an opinion may express not only critical confusion but historical misinformation; if *The Death of a Salesman*, for example, faces truth honestly and with appropriate art, it is tragedy in a long recognized tradition, and nothing in the tradition requires that Willy Loman comprehend what the dramatist reveals. It is the actual point of his play that a mode of life can produce an understanding so disordered that it cannot perceive its disorder. This, it will be recalled, is also the point of *Coriolanus*. If, without other changes, Shakespeare had written that play in the style of *Othello* or *Macbeth*, the tragic vision, the victory of insight over defeat, would still have been absent in the hero but its presence in the play would never have been doubted.

[11] If we assume, for the reasons Mr. Krutch gave, that tragedy is dead, the following situation would be instructive, or at least interesting: Suppose a modern dramatist should write a very good play based upon the idea that we can no longer view men on the scale of tragedy. Would not the hero attain tragic stature by facing this idea honestly and intelligently, even if he granted its truth? Or, if he failed to perceive the idea at all, could not the play, which significantly conveyed it, still have the quality of tragedy? I merely suggest that, although a mature conclusion that tragedy is dead would inhibit the reading and writing of further tragedy, it might well remain in itself a subject of tragedy.

xi. Some conclusions

ALTHOUGH the interpretations found here may be less conventional than otherwise, I have enjoyed being a little old-fashioned in a concern for Shakespeare's characters. The fanciful, indwelling Richard II has been seen as something of a realist, although a devious one, and in this role he serves to establish another character as he explicitly frames what the tacit Bolingbroke seems to conceal even from himself. Henry cannot declare his own motives until events, and Richard, speak for him. Iago has been examined for his perverse tendency to believe in fantasy he constructs for the injury of others. The fall of Othello has been explained partly by his "assumption" of Iago's role and partly by his impulse to depersonalize himself in ritual, a motive also present with less delusion in Brutus. Macbeth's fate as divided man has been found in his perception of evil on the one hand and "rapt" drift into evil on the other. Hamlet has been the subject of three essays. The first has dealt with his conflict between deficiency and excess of passion, the second with his concern for privacy of mind, and the third with his desire for privacy as the motive for a feigned madness which is both complex and ambiguous.

I have also considered character study from the stand-point of tradition, and in doing so have tried to solve some problems arising from past interpretation and from the ex-perience of many readers. One such problem is the conflict between psychological and antipsychological interpretation of *Othello*. I have agreed with those who doubt motivation which prepares Othello, as a character, for the debacle of III.iii, but I have disagreed with skeptical tradition by find-ing that psychological motives, explicit in Iago and implicit in the reputation theme, prepare the audience for Othello's action. His inevitable fall in the temptation scene does not stem from what he has been but from what the play has been, from prevailing traits of several characters which estab-lish a theme. In addition, I have tried to enlarge the issue by stressing motivation which appears not before but after the temptation scene as Othello dedicates himself to ritual and symbol.

Further traditional character problems have been encoun-tered, of course, in *Hamlet*. A hero who thinks too precisely on the event but who meets events with surpassing action is a paradox issuing not so much from Coleridge as from scholars anxious to admit two Hamlets in a single play, one of them a melodramatic figure derived from the sources and the other a Shakespearian character who is admittedly overreflective. If we find, however, that Shakespeare stressed Hamlet's emotive involvement far more than his pale thought there will be no conflict between character and action, for a sense of inappropriate emotion can accompany decisive ac-tion with full consistency. Hamlet's antic disposition pre-sents another question. In discussing it I have tried to show that Shakespeare altered the old motive to suit his new play; if we understand Hamlet as assuming the antic role not to protect his person (as in the sources) but mainly to isolate himself from recorder players, the feigned madness need no longer puzzle us. It will still serve to alarm rather than quiet Claudius, but it will also serve Hamlet's inner necessity.

In discussing Shakespeare's characters one is expected, and sometimes tempted, to deal unduly with cause and effect. Certain queries seem inevitable. What is there about Othello which leads him to ritual as an expression of delusion? How did Hamlet come to sense that he lacked passion? When these questions refer to a character's life before the play begins, they can be dismissed, but they deserve an answer when they are addressed to the text. It would not be irresponsible, for example, to say that Othello assumes a ritual role because formal conduct is part of the military code, or that Hamlet is unsure in emotion because an object of love, his mother, has become unworthy. In each instance the play can carry the explanation. But it can also support several different motives, and it seems to me that a choice among them should be left to the reader. Hamlet's deficiency-in-excess of emotion is announced by Hamlet, it has a cumulative development, and it is a psychological conflict which can be recognized by anyone as part of his experience. The critic should point this out and he may, but need not, specify causal origins and relationships.[1] Of these there are a number; it must be granted that they are important and that one who dismisses them in order to read *Hamlet* "for fun" probably gets very little fun from thinking. The assumption I have made, however, is that thinking people are happier if they are given the material for thought and allowed to think.

[1] Or he may specify an inclusive philosophy, if he believes that the play contains and discloses it.

Although a psychological and moral approach to Shakespeare underlies this book, very little of the critical method
belongs to that tradition. Motivation has been seen as the
function of all parts of a play, and never simply as an ac-
cumulation of traits derived from the words and acts of a
character. In *Julius Caesar* the element of rite and ceremony
is introduced as an expositional theme which has no relation
at first to Brutus; later, at the appropriate moment, this
theme serves as a concrete means of expressing his moral
conflict. The assassination is then staged as a formal sacrifice
instead of in the manner of Plutarch who compared the
dying Caesar to a beast taken by hunters. Finally, Antony
not only uses counterceremony for his ends but consistently
reverses the vision of Brutus so that the dish carved for the
gods becomes more and more the carcass hewn for hounds.
The unity of character and theme in *Julius Caesar* is simple
when compared with that of *Hamlet, Othello,* or *Macbeth.*
In these plays the central character's state of mind is reflected so constantly and so variously in the accompanying
themes that psychological consistency grows beyond consistency of character to become a unity of the whole. When
Hamlet, for example, assumes his antic disposition a similar
quality, hitherto absent, is assumed by the Ghost, Polonius,
and the greater part of Elsinore; the play in large measure
puts on the antic disposition.

Interpretation which views character as a function of
poetic drama implies a rejection of naturalism or the ex-
ternals of realism. When Othello kneels with Iago under the
heavenly light which then becomes a symbol around which
he constructs a ritual of death and purification, any linkage
of his behavior with our day-to-day life becomes indirect.

The indirection, however, is that of art in which remoteness increases immediacy. If Brutus' ceremony of bathing his arms in Caesar's blood tells us more about him than does his quarrel with Cassius, or if Macbeth's great incantation beginning "Come seeling night/ Scarf up the eye of pitiful day," reveals him more aptly than do his confessions of ambition, Brutus and Macbeth become "distant" symbolic figures. To regard them in such situations as men, the unconscious practice of much character study, is to consider them either unreal or psychotic. I do not wish to develop this point; it is a recognized one which arouses opposition only when actually applied. But it can diminish disagreement. My emphasis, for example, of the Hamlet-Laertes quarrel at Ophelia's grave may cause disapproval because it points to something shrill, violent, or indecorous as a final expression of Hamlet's conflict. Those who find this disturbing will possibly do so because they view Hamlet's excess as that of a realistic character. It should not be so viewed. If at the funeral of a girl he loved the hero of a realistic novel were to quarrel at the grave with her brother, he should excite a morbid or clinical interest. The heightened, mythic figure who behaves in that fashion excites no morbidity and is never clinical, for a tradition which is very old entitles him to represent normal crises through excessive and stylized behavior. I do not believe that my reliance upon this idea has been inconsistent with the treatment of any play.[2]

[2] On the surface, it might appear that this principle contradicts the interpretation of Hamlet's antic disposition in Chapter VII. In other words, it might be said that if Hamlet simply represents normal crises through excessive and stylized behavior, then his excesses cannot represent unbalance or "ecstasy" as they would in a realistic character. If we may not interpret Hamlet's brawl with Laertes as we would the conduct of a "real" character, then are we permitted to see it as an indication of

Nor does the Shakespearian mythic character need discursive motivation, any more than Pandora or Lot's wife
need built-up explanations for their fatal curiosity. There
should be no uneasiness over the assumption by Othello in
III.iii of a role previously foreign to him if the new role
accords with a theme which controls the play. Similarly, no
concern should arise from Macbeth's quick submission to a
supernatural spell of raptness so long as the spell dominates
the action and thus affects not only Macbeth but the reader
or spectator as well. These remarks may appear to question
the psychological substance of Shakespeare's art, but they
actually vindicate it. Only when themes such as reputation
in *Othello* or raptness in *Macbeth* are found to color entire
plays instead of individual characters, and only when the
individual character is understood as largely symbolic, will
the psychological content of Shakespeare take on full meaning.[3] Shakespeare's characters may be related to Pandora or

genuine unbalance, as we would if it were the excessive behavior of a
real person? I must answer that my interpretation of the antic disposition
is not based upon such an inference. I have not reasoned, for example,
that because Hamlet's conduct in the Queen's closet scene is excessive, it
is therefore an indication of genuine ecstasy carried past the point of
feigning. Rather, I have made the point that Hamlet's behavior in this
scene, and in others which are similar, is repeatedly the *same* as it is in
situations of clearly feigned madness. The feigning scenes establish a norm,
if it may be called that, of aberrant behavior. This, then, becomes the
standard, the convention, by which ecstasy is measured in the play; and
when Hamlet's acts and words in a nonfeigning situation become pointedly indistinguishable from those he elsewhere employs while feigning, a
dramatically clear ambiguity results. Excessive action or speech, as such,
has little to do with the problem.

As for other instances, the excessive behavior of Richard II, Hamlet
(Chap. V), Antony, and Cleopatra is made clear and significant within
the play. This is done by commentary of other characters, contrast, or
direct self-revelation. The stylized action of Brutus and Othello is pointed
up as ritual within the normally stylized medium.

[3] The principle behind this statement is implicit, of course, in the better
modern treatments of motivation in Shakespeare. For a study which makes

Lot's wife but they transcend these figures of myth because the plays in which they appear establish complex moods which are pertinent to their actions. Sometimes they are discursively and causally motivated (Brutus), and sometimes they are not (Othello), but the scale of psychological meaning is unconnected with the discursive element or lack of it. Both Brutus and Othello represent the tragedy of ceremonial delusion, but Othello in the later and nondiscursive play is the better representation because the poetry and stagecraft are better; the dedication under the light of heaven, the persistence of the light as a symbol, and the incantation of the death scene, excel any similar elements in *Julius Caesar*.

The psychological themes we have examined bear upon the nature of Shakespearian tragedy. As we follow the protagonists in their fated careers a common quality of withdrawal into self seems to distinguish them. This quality is rarely sentimental,[4] but it is always willful or perverse. Richard II withdraws to mirror-worship and expresses it in pageants of defeat and martyrdom; Brutus becomes self-sufficient in ritual which enables him to abide the role of conspirator and executioner; Othello follows the same course, emphasizing as did Brutus the motive of hateless sacrifice; Hamlet rejects the world as a sterile promontory, proceeds to stress motives of privacy with the alien antic, and becomes engrossed in testing his capacity for balanced

---

it effectively explicit, see J. I. M. Stewart, *Character and Motivation in Shakespeare: Some Recent Appraisals Examined* (London, 1949).

[4] Professor A. H. R. Fairchild looks upon the tragic heroes as sentimentalists. *Shakespeare and the Tragic Theme*, in *University of Missouri Studies*, Vol. XIX, No. 2 (1944). He remarks (p. 111), "Egoism and self-pity comprise the third mark of the sentimental mind." My interpretation would recognize the egoism, but little of the self-pity.

passion; Macbeth is not merely withdrawn but is translated into "brainsickly" raptness; Antony, the most naturalistic of the major figures becomes detached in sensuality; Lear, Timon, and Coriolanus all retreat into egoism, and Lear is the only one of the three who "returns."

So far it would appear simply that Shakespeare's tragic heroes isolate themselves from other men. But this simple truth can be our starting point in considering the form, the manner, of the isolation as it appears in plays we have studied. Retreat into self is generally marked by ceremonial: pageant, ritual, incantation, or play-acting, either singly or in combination. The return of the outer world is often presented as a breaking of the ceremonial spell. Richard II's last pageant is the deposition scene during which he compels Bolingbroke to join him in holding the crown and calls for the symbolic looking glass that he may better witness his own fall. His shattering of the glass ends the pose, and the scene turns to realism. The ritual withdrawal of Brutus is ended by Antony in a mock-ritual and a depiction of the sacrifice, the dish carved for the gods, in the very guise which Brutus disavowed—the carcass hewn for hounds. Othello's retirement into self, also climaxed in a sacrifice, is suddenly ended by Emilia in Shakespeare's most dramatic clash between the formal and realistic planes of being. Macbeth's incantatory retreat into darkness, sleep, and raptness is at its height in the episode of Duncan's murder, and the drunken porter breaks the spell with comic symbols of contradiction.

Hamlet does not appear to fit this plan until we note that he identifies himself with the "passion's slave" theme as he recites and hears lines from an archaic, ritualized tragedy; [5]

[5] The actual "passion's slave" speech to Horatio comes later.

the identification then grows as he dwells upon the art of acting in his lines to the players. It is also significant that he lapses finally into the extremes of emotion during a scene in which he watches the "maimed rites" of Ophelia. Here he at once celebrates and desecrates his own flaw or "mole of nature" when he challenges Laertes to formal exchange of passion, and his deed thus matches Richard's breaking of the glass at the moment of dethronement. Hamlet's antic disposition is also marked by ceremony. It begins at the swearing of secrecy, during which there is repeated insistence upon ritual, and its appearance throughout the play is usually stylized; Hamlet can neither bait Polonius nor withdraw to contemplate recorders with Rosencrantz and Guildenstern without suggesting the ceremonious, half in derision and half in self-realization.

Antony and Cleopatra is the final example. Here isolation takes form as the chief characters cast themselves in the formal roles of orthodox tragedy. The "nobleness of life" is consciously asserted and reasserted, and the *de casibus* "symposium" in V.i immediately precedes Cleopatra's vision, with its dolphin image, of the flawed hero. Her dream of Antony is promptly diminished by Dolabella, and in the next scene the Seleucus affair turns Cleopatra's claim of tragedy for herself (pity for the "fall" of "the greatest") into something close to travesty.

Naturally, the use of ritual or other artifice in the expression of withdrawal does not fit the whole of Shakespearian tragedy, but it is both characteristic and prominent. What does this mean? We may reject two inferences immediately: that Shakespeare disapproved of ceremony as such, and that he questioned his own artistic medium which was formalized

drama. Some will say, of course, that we must reject all
inferences because stylized scenes can have no meaning
within a stylized play. I have considered this objection care-
fully, however, and believe that it ignores a principle which
is both historical and critical. Formal elements can be, and
are, presented within a formal medium; the play-within-
a-play is the standard illustration. And I believe that a
checking of examples will show that the attitudes which
express delusive withdrawal are stylized in a way which
distinguishes them from the ordinary formal context. If this
is true we are free to consider the implications.

Without wishing to complicate Shakespeare's "moral universe," I suggest that he knew the idea of tragedy to be
capable of tragic misuse, that he saw the elevation to tragic
dignity of an erring protagonist as something which could
be turned into the elevation of error itself. It is just this
transformation which most of the heroes attempt for themselves. As Richard II invents his pageants of martyrdom, as
Brutus and Othello enter upon rites of self-justification, as
Macbeth incants the spell of his own helplessness before
evil, each in effect composes spurious tragedy for himself,
casts himself as a fated victim bound to do evil which is
not really evil because it is made beautiful with gesture,
intonation, and invocation.[6] This is not the tragedy Shakespeare composes but a delusion of tragedy entertained by the
protagonist; it is the false tragic sense which emerges as
false upon appearance of the genuine, for as the true vision
becomes clear the untrue is formulated and rejected.
Othello's self-contrived ritual tragedy ends with the sacrifice

[6] No one, I hope, will read this as meaning that these "tragedies" are
spurious *because* they are ritualized, or that ritual is a dubious ingredient
in tragedy. On the contrary, it is an essential.

killing; Shakespeare's tragedy of Othello ends when Emilia tells the truth about the sacrifice and Othello understands it. Richard II sees the mirror ritual in the deposition scene as the true expression of his fall; Shakespeare modifies this *de casibus* pose by Richard's breaking of the glass, an act which discloses the erstwhile master of ceremony as a servant of egoistic passion. In this scheme of things *Antony and Cleopatra* would become Shakespeare's terminal expression of the principle. There, the protagonists actually declare their own claims to tragic stature, and the ironical but sympathetic exposure of this pseudo-tragedy is conscious and explicit.

There is a further and perhaps a broader way in which one theme we have studied reflects the nature of Shakespearian tragedy. And in this instance it raises questions which extend beyond Shakespeare. In the chapter on *Antony and Cleopatra* the role of "diminished" protagonist became an issue related not only to currents of the past but to those of our own time, during which the problem of an ironically reduced hero has led to various doubts about the tragic quality of modern literature. There is no need here to summarize the discussion in Chapter X, but I should not wish a concluding statement to lack mention of two suggestions to be found there: first, that the diminished hero is not without historical foundation in the writing of tragedy, and second, that tragedy of any period, past or present, has communicated a necessary sense of stature through the play itself as often as through the protagonist.

The study of a playwright's themes with respect to motivation, structure, and meaning leads to a final question. How did his art begin, change, and grow? We might expect to find in the earlier *Romeo and Juliet* or *Richard II* far less control of thematic materials than in the later *Macbeth* or *Othello*. Such a conclusion, however, is far from warranted, which is surprising because skill in joining theme with setting, character, and plot would seem to develop only after long experience. I do not suggest that the earlier efforts are equal to the great tragedies, but I believe they contain the qualities we have considered in a form which is already definitive.

Working in nonchronological order, I began a study of the "haste" theme in *Romeo and Juliet* after writing the essays on *Hamlet* and *Julius Caesar*. I expected to find in the earlier tragedy a tendency to let lines recite the theme as a mere accompaniment of plot, with very little interaction between thematic and structural elements. That this surmise was wrong is implied clearly by the chapter on *Romeo and Juliet*, for Shakespeare ventures far beyond simple dialogue upon haste within a haste-ridden tragedy. We find, for example, that fluid speed is managed by the "run-on" device which ends one scene with a specific statement of the haste theme, and begins the next on a variation of the same statement. Other thematic effects, moreover, are secured at the same time. Act I, scene iv begins with maskers who speak plainly of rejecting slow "prologues"; it brings Mercutio onstage as an embodiment of speed and nimbleness; and it introduces a note of concern over late arrival at the feast. In a choric speech Romeo then contrasts this late arrival with the earliness, or untimeliness, of the tragedy he senses in the offing. At this, the haste theme is converted to action with Benvolio's "Strike, drum" and the quick march of the maskers. The run-on device is then used to introduce the next scene which starts with Capulet servants preparing in chaotic haste for the feast itself. We may compare this remarkable thematic plan with one of a dozen years later. In *Macbeth* (II.i, ii, and iii) is to be found a unity of theme with other elements which is possibly unequalled in Shakespeare. In Chapter IX this was described as a statement of theme in one scene, conversion of theme to action in the next, fluid connection of scene with scene by thematic carry-over, and continual interplay between theme and character. It is interesting that the portion of *Romeo and Juliet* we have just reviewed shows all of these elements in similar coordination. The *Macbeth* achievement is, of course, the greater one but its superiority lies not so much in the structural control of theme as in poetic quality.

A similar comparison may be made between *Macbeth* and the much earlier *Richard II*. Reference to the chapters on these two plays will show that in *Macbeth* the episode of Banquo's death repeats the thematic and psychological plan used in presenting the murder of Duncan. A like process, however, appears in *Richard II* when the pattern of the Flint Castle scene is skillfully followed in the scene of Richard's deposition. This, it may be recalled, led in Chapter III to the conclusion that *Richard II* shows an early mastery by Shakespeare of a difficult art, the combining of plot, character revelation, and idea in a scheme of parallel episodes.

Detailed comparison could be extended, but I believe it would point to the same result. The plan of ritual scenes in *Othello* is more complex than that of *Julius Caesar*, but it is not remarkably better simply as a plan; the ritual theme in *Othello* is superior mainly because the poetic medium has been heightened. *Hamlet* and *Richard II* could also be con-

trasted. Had Shakespeare written both at the same level of
style it is doubtful that *Hamlet* would still be the better of
the two, for the combining of plot, character, and idea in
Richard II shows, if anything, greater unity and concentration. So far as the matters we have studied are concerned,
Shakespeare learned the fundamentals of his art quickly and
early. As he proceeded, the plays became unquestionably
richer in quality but his ability to turn theme and idea into
dramatic art became established with *Romeo and Juliet* and
Richard II.

Index

Romeo (*Romeo and Juliet*): role in haste theme, 10, 12-20, 24-25; problem of tragic stature, 187, 189

Romeo and Juliet: haste theme in, 10-25, 204-5; problem of as a tragedy, 187-192; thematic plan in, 204-5, 206

Rosaline (*Romeo and Juliet*), 17

Rosenberg, Marvin, 117*n*

Rosencrantz (*Hamlet*): role in recorder theme, 75, 84, 85, 105; role in antic theme, 100, 101

Ross (*Macbeth*), 150

Sampson (*Romeo and Juliet*), 10

Scarus (*Antony and Cleopatra*), 171

Schanzer, Ernest, 41*n*

Schücking, L. L., 71*n*, 116*n*-117*n*

Scroop (*Richard II*), 30, 31

Seleucus (*Antony and Cleopatra*), 181-82, 183, 184

Sexual infatuation: as a tragic theme in *Antony and Cleopatra*, 157-184, 184-92 *passim*

Shaw, G. B.: on *Antony and Cleopatra*, 157-58, 181

Sleep theme (*Macbeth*), 139-56

Sleepwalking scene (*Macbeth*): themes of play in, 140, 154-55

Spencer, Hazelton, 87

Stein, Arnold, 141*n*

Stewart, Charles D., 62*n*

Stewart, J. I. M., 199*n*

Stirling, Alice, vii

Stoll, E. E., vii, 117*n*

Structure: definition of in discussion, 3

Tannenbaum, S. A., 114*n*

Temptation scene (*Othello*), 117-23

Theme: meaning of term in discussion, 3-4, 83; evolution of Shakespeare's capacity to present, 203-6

Three Plays for Puritans (G. B. Shaw), 157

Thyreus (*Antony and Cleopatra*), 172

Tillyard, E. M. W., vii

Timon (*Timon of Athens*), 187-88, 189, 200

Timon of Athens, 186-87, 188, 189-90

Tragedy: problem of in *Antony and Cleopatra*, 157-92; stature required of, 184-92; observations on Shakespearian, 199-203, and *passim*

Tybalt (*Romeo and Juliet*), 15

Van Doren, Mark, 140*n*

Volumnia (*Coriolanus*), 187*n*

Walker, Roy, 61*n*-62*n*, 66*n*, 71*n*, 140*n*

Wilson, J. Dover, 35*n*, 67*n*, 77*n*

York (*Richard II*), 28-29, 30, 31, 32-33